NATIONALISM, COLONIALISM, AND LITERATURE

NATIONALISM, COLONIALISM, AND LITERATURE

TERRY EAGLETON
FREDRIC JAMESON
EDWARD W. SAID

Introduction by
SEAMUS DEANE

A Field Day Company Book

University of Minnesota Press
Minneapolis
London

Published by the University of Minnesota Press
111 Third Avenue South, Suite 290, Minneapolis, MN 55401-2520
Printed in the United States of America on acid-free paper
Fourth printing, 1997

Library of Congress Cataloging-in-Publication Data

Nationalism, colonialism, and literature / Terry Eagleton, Fredric
Jameson, and Edward W. Said ; introduction by Seamus Deane.
p.   cm.
"These essays were originally published as pamphlets by Field
Day Theatre Company"—Pref.
Contents: Nationalism—irony and commitment / Terry Eagleton—
Modernism and imperialism / Fredric Jameson—Yeats and
decolonization / Edward W. Said.
ISBN 0-8166-1862-3.—ISBN 0-8166-1863-1 (pbk.)
1. English literature—Irish authors—History and criticism.
2. Yeats, W. B. (William Butler), 1865–1939—Criticism and
interpretation.   3. Joyce, James, 1882–1941—Criticism and
interpretation.   4. Nationalism in literature.   5. Colonies in
literature.   6. Ireland in literature.   7. Nationalism—Ireland.
I. Eagleton, Terry, 1943– Nationalism—irony and commitment.
1990.   II. Jameson, Fredric. Modernization and imperialism.   1990.
III. Said, Edward W.   Yeats and decolonization.   1990.   IV. Field
Day Theatre Company.
PR8753.N38   1990
820-9′358—dc20   90-10855

CONTENTS

INTRODUCTION 3
Seamus Deane

NATIONALISM:
IRONY AND COMMITMENT 23
Terry Eagleton

MODERNISM AND
IMPERIALISM 43
Fredric Jameson

YEATS AND
DECOLONIZATION 69
Edward W. Said

INDEX 99

NATIONALISM, COLONIALISM, AND LITERATURE

INTRODUCTION

SEAMUS DEANE

The three essays presented here have in common with one another and with the Field Day enterprise the conviction that we need a new discourse for a new relationship between our idea of the human subject and our idea of human communities. What is now happening in Ireland, most especially in Northern Ireland (constitutionally an integral part of the United Kingdom), is only one of the many crises that have made the need for such a discourse peremptory. In Africa, South America, the Middle East, the Soviet Union, and Eastern Europe, the nature of the crisis is more glaringly exposed and its consequences seem both more ominous and far-reaching in their effects. Nevertheless, the Irish-English collision has its own importance. Ireland is the only Western European country that has had both an early and a late colonial experience. Out of that, Ireland produced, in the first three decades of this century, a remarkable literature in which the attempt to overcome and replace the colonial experience by something other, something that would be "native" and yet not provincial, was a dynamic and central energy. The ultimate failure of that attempt to imagine a truly liberating cultural alternative is as well known as the brilliance of the initial effort. Now that the established system has again been called into question, even to the point where it must seriously alter or collapse, Irish writing, operating in the shadow or in the wake of the earlier attempt, has once more raised the question of how the individual subject can be envisaged in relation to its community, its past history, and a possible future.

Terry Eagleton's analysis of nationalism identifies the radical contradictions that necessarily beset it. The oppositional terms it deploys are the very terms it must ultimately abolish. Yet such abolition is not an easy, peremptory gesture. The divisions of English and Irish, Protestant and Catholic, must be lived through in the present. It is, therefore, necessary to sustain commitment to them under the aegis of irony. Otherwise the oppressive conditions they bespeak will merely be reproduced. In Europe the category of the aesthetic has as its project the reconciliation of the specific and the universal. This has no application in Ireland, where the radical and abstract Enlightenment view of the individual and the regionalist particularity of nineteenth-century Irish nationalism remain discrete, with no totalizing vision that can contain or conciliate them. This is true even when we consider Joyce's writings where the totalizing process finally homogenizes difference, erases rather than lives through oppositions like those of the cosmopolitan versus the national community. Any politics that has a transformative power has to envisage, if in a negative way, the freedom and self-autonomy that would make such politics unnecessary. This is not merely a theoretical paradox. It is a condition that has to be passionately lived.

Fredric Jameson's essay pursues the contradiction, explored in his other works, between the limited experience of the individual and the dispersed conditions that govern it. In any imperial system, the subject, living in the home country, does not have any living access to the far-flung system that makes his or her subjective existence possible. Jameson argues that the attempt to achieve some coordination between private existence and the global, institutional apparatus of imperialism has been the stimulus behind many of the experimental forms assumed by modern literature. Joyce's experiments in representation and his dismantling of its traditional forms and assumptions are, for Jameson, a particularly telling example of the way in which a closed society, like Dublin, still available to the individual consciousness as an autonomous culture, has had to envisage its relationship with a metropolitan and imperial center like London as a paralyzed, even catatonic condition. It has no motor force of its own. It is subject to agencies beyond its control and therefore imperfectly known or realized— the British and Roman Catholic imperial world systems. Reading Joyce against an English writer like Forster, Jameson discloses the reasons for Joyce's disintegration of the monadic subject of the bourgeois novel. Forster's failure to do so is not merely a formal failure; it bespeaks the failure of the political creed of liberalism, with its peculiarly intense valorization of the autonomous human subject and its consequent failure either to apprehend or to comprehend the operations of the system that initially gave birth to it and that ultimately undermines it.

Edward Said concentrates on Yeats, seeing his work as an exemplary and early instance of the process of decolonization, the liberation of the poet's community from its inbred and oppressive servility to a new, potentially revolutionary condition. The Yeats that other colonial countries experience is not necessarily the Yeats Ireland experiences now. For, although he did perhaps fall in the end into a blind provincialism, his attempt to escape from the thrall of Ireland's mutilating nineteenth-century experience has been reproduced and developed in other countries and cultures since. The asphyxiating aspects of a regional nativism, although they persist in his work and become more pronounced in its later phases, do not obliterate its radically liberating elements. These have been imitated and transcended in the writings of African, Palestinian, and South American writers who have read Yeats as a poet whose re-creation of himself and his community provides a model for their own projects—the giving of a voice and a history to those who have been deprived of the consciousness of both.

These essays were originally published as pamphlets by Field Day Theatre Company, which was founded in 1980 when the present political crisis in Northern Ireland was already twelve years old. That crisis continues and shows every sign of prolonging itself for a considerable length of time. Field Day is a response to that situation. It is based in Derry (or Londonderry), the second city in Northern Ireland; six of its seven directors are from the North and all of its enterprises, in theater, in pamphlets, and in the Field Day Anthology of Irish Writing (1990) have a bearing upon the nature and genesis of the present impasse. Although Northern Ireland is the site of the conflict, the whole island, including the Republic of Ireland, is involved as is the United Kingdom.

Field Day's analysis of the situation derives from the conviction that it is, above all, a colonial crisis. This is not a popular view in the political and academic establishment in Ireland. Historians in particular have been engaged for more than twenty years in what is referred to as a revision of Irish history, the chief aim of which was to demolish the nationalist mythology that had been in place for over fifty years, roughly from 1916 to 1966. This polemical ambition has been in large part realized. The nationalist narrative, which told the story of seven hundred years of English misrule (finally brought to a conclusion by the heroic rebellion of 1916 and the violence of the following six years, and now culminating in the unfinished business of the North), has lost much of its appeal and legitimacy save for those who are committed to the IRA and the armed struggle. Revisionism defends itself against those who describe it as simply another orthodoxy, created in accord with the political circumstances of the moment, by claiming to have revealed such a degree of complexity in Irish and Anglo-Irish affairs that no systematic explanation is possible. It has effectively localized interpretation, confining it within groups, interests, classes, and periods; any attempt to see these issues as variations on a ghostly paradigm, like colonialism, is characterized as "ideological" and, on that account, is doomed. Ultimately, there may have been no such thing as colonialism. It is, according to many historians, one of the phantoms created by nationalism, which is itself phantasmal enough.

Field Day regards this new orthodoxy with disfavor because it shows little or no capacity for self-analysis. Its own demolition of nationalism rebounds on itself. Moreover, it has paid no serious attention to the realm of culture, regarding it as in some sense separate from politics. In this it has been supported by many who still believe in the autonomy of cultural artifacts, and who, as a consequence, subscribe to the Arnoldian notion that the work of art that most successfully disengages itself from the particularities of its origin and production is, by virtue of that "disengagement," most fully and purely itself. It is "universal," the proper thing for art to be. Contrastingly, Field Day sees art as a specific activity indeed, but one in which the whole history of a culture is deeply inscribed. The interpretation of culture is not predicated on the notion that there is some universal quality or essence that culture alone can successfully pursue and capture. That is itself a political idea that has played a crucial role in Irish experience. One of Field Day's particular aims has been to expose the history and function of that idea and to characterize its disfiguring effects.

To do so, it has been necessary to engage again with the concept of nationalism. It is not, in the Irish context, an exclusively Irish phenomenon, for the island has now, particularly in the North, and has had for at least two hundred years, British nationalism as a predominant political and cultural influence. In fact, Irish nationalism is, in its foundational moments, a derivative of its British counterpart. Almost all nationalist movements have been derided as provincial, actually or potentially racist, given to exclusivist and doctrinaire positions and rhetoric. These descriptions fit British nationalism perfectly, as the contemporaries of any of its exponents on Ireland—Edmund Spenser, Sir John Davies, Sir William Temple, Coleridge, Carlyle, Arnold, Enoch Powell, Ian Paisley—will prove. The point about Irish nationalism, the features within it that have prevented it from being a movement toward liberation, is that it is, *mutatis mutandis*, a copy of that by which it felt itself to be oppressed. The collusion of Irish with British nationalism has produced contrasting stereotypes whose most destructive effect has been the laying of the cultural basis for religious sectarianism. It is perhaps stating the obvious to say that the competing nationalisms have always defined themselves in relation to either Protestantism or Catholicism. Every attempt to refuse that definition—by the United Irishmen in the late eighteenth century, by the trades union movement in the early twentieth century—has been defeated by ruthless and concerted efforts. We are not witnessing in Northern Ireland some outmoded battle between religious sects that properly belong to the seventeenth century. We are witnessing rather the effects of a contemporary colonialism that has retained and developed an ideology of dominance and subservience within the readily available idiom of religious division. Constitutionally, as Northern Ireland reminds us, Britain is a specifically Protestant country. That constitutional "anachronism"—with its roots in London and its rank flowering in Belfast—is a political reality when the constitution is challenged.

All nationalisms have a metaphysical dimension, for they are all driven by an ambition to realize their intrinsic essence in some specific and tangible form. The form may be a political structure or a literary tradition. Although the problems created by such an ambition are sufficiently intractable in themselves, they are intensified to the point of absurdity when a nationalist self-conception imagines itself to be the ideal model to which all others should conform.

Seamus Deane

That is a characteristic of colonial and imperial nations. Because they universalize themselves, they regard any insurgency against them as necessarily provincial. In response, insurgent nationalisms attempt to create a version of history for themselves in which their intrinsic essence has always manifested itself, thereby producing readings of the past that are as monolithic as that which they are trying to supplant. They are usually, as in Ireland, under the additional disadvantage that much of their past has been destroyed, silenced, erased. Therefore, the amalgam they produce is susceptible to attack and derision.

Nevertheless, nationalism of both kinds has been particularly effective in the modern period precisely because it contains within itself this metaphysical essentialism. It has been able, on that account, to tell a characteristically modern (or modernist) story, with a power and persuasiveness that even yet have appeal. The story is, in effect, the story of the fall of modern humankind from a state of bliss into the peculiarly modern condition of alienation. The imperial nationalism of Britain told this tale over and over in a series of brilliant and ingenious parables that sought to identify that originary moment of decline. In literary history, from Coleridge to Arnold to Eliot and Leavis, the new narrative rediscovered a seventeenth-century Eden with a subsequent decline that had come to a culmination in the present. In the novel, Conrad, Kipling, Ford, Forster, and Lawrence brooded upon the failure of Englishness in imperial and other foreign territories. Imperial nativism sought solace in time past for the problems of the present and often came up with the notion that present failure was the consequence of the decline of "national character," perhaps the most enduring and insubstantial creation of all nationalist mythologies. In Ireland, just at this time undergoing its literary revival, the Edenic moment was displaced back into the pre-Christian (and therefore presectarian) past, and the model figures that emerged as types of Irish identity were, of necessity, legendary—like Cuchalain—and, by nature, susceptible to almost any reformulation. The central point here is, that it was in the late years of the nineteenth and early years of the twentieth century that the political situations in Britain and in Ireland demanded a reconstituted version of both the national characters and the literary traditions of each. This is one—but a crucial—example of the interaction between the political and cultural zones and of the interaction between the British and the Irish that has done so much to produce the present complex and stymied situation in which we find ourselves.

In previous pamphlets, Field Day has attempted to come to terms with this inherited situation by demonstrating that the interweave of political and cultural (largely literary) forces is now subject to a fresh analysis, stimulated by the pressure of the existing political crisis. It is a truism to say that no language is innocent. It is more difficult to trace, within the rhetorics of political and literary discourses, the forms and varieties of incrimination, subjection, insurgency, evasion, and stereotyping that determine or are determined by our past and present interpretations. It seemed to us that, by doing so, we could begin to reverse the effects of the colonialism that has wrought such devastating as well as subtle effects in Ireland and in the consciousness of its people.

At its most powerful, colonialism is a process of radical dispossession. A colonized people is without a specific history and even, as in Ireland and other cases, without a specific language. The recovery from the lost Irish language has taken the form of an almost vengeful virtuosity in the English language, an attempt to make Irish English a language in its own right rather than an adjunct to English itself. The virtuosity of early modern Irish writing and its hesitant relationship to the language revival movement exemplify this queasy condition. Yeats, Joyce, and Synge present its characteristic features most fully, but others do so in only slightly less complete array—Wilde, George Moore, Shaw, and Beckett. But the linguistic question, although important, seemed secondary to the question of repossession—that is to say, the repossession of these (and other) authors for an interpretation that was governed by a reading of the conditions in which their work was produced and in the Irish conditions in which it was read. It was inevitable that Yeats and Joyce would initially take most of our attention, since it was they, more than anyone else, who had been (mis)read in the light of what was understood to be English or British literature, international modernism, the plight of humankind in the twentieth century. Our reading of them was designed to restore them to the culture in which they were still alive as presences, to interpret the interpretations that mediated them for us, to repossess their revolutionary and authoritative force for the here and now of the present in Ireland.

There is an inevitable monotony involved here, inescapable in colonial conditions. What seems like an endless search for a lost communal or even personal identity is doubly futile. Just naming it indicates that it is lost; once named, it can never be unnamed. In the second place, such an identity is wholly unreal. It can be made manifest only by pretending that it is the conclusion to a search of which it was the origin. When Yeats invented an Irish literary tradition in the English language, he did not discover in Swift, Burke, and others the Protestant Irish essence for which he sought; he sought in them the essence that he then discovered. The same is true of versions of English literature that find in Shakespeare and in Keats a native English genius that is somehow deflected in Milton or Pope. The pursuit of such questions leads to notions of national character, questions of the language appropriate to its proper expression and, by extension, to the stereotyping of groups, classes, races in relation to the kinds of writing (or music, architecture, whatever it may be) that they produce. Still, monotonous as it may be, it is inescapable. Otherwise we may never see the colonial forest for the nativist trees.

In the attempted discovery of its "true" identity, a community often begins with the demolition of the false stereotypes within which it has been entrapped. This is an intricate process, since the stereotypes are successful precisely because they have been interiorized. They are not merely impositions from the colonizer on the colonized. It is a matter of common knowledge that stereotypes are mutually generative of each other, as in the case of the English and the Irish. Although the stereotyping initiative, so to speak, is taken by the community that exercises power, it has to create a stereotype of itself as much as it does of others. Indeed, this is one of the ways by which otherness is defined. The definition of otherness, the degree to which others can be persuasively shown to be discordant with the putative norm, provides a rationale for conquest. The Irish reluctance to yield to the caricature of themselves as barbarous or uncivilized exposed the nullity of the English rationale although it also aggravated the ferocity of the process of subjugation. But within the last one hundred years the terms of the exchange altered. In all kinds of places—in Renan, in Arnold, in Havelock Ellis, in the career of George Bernard Shaw—it was quite suddenly revealed that the English national character was defective and in need of the Irish, or Celtic, character in order to supplement it and enable it to survive. All the theorists of racial degeneration—Galton, Nordau, Lombroso, Spengler—shared with literary critics and poets and novelists the conviction that the decline of the West must be halted by some infusion or transfusion of energy from an "unspoiled" source. The Irish seemed to qualify for English purposes. They were white, rural, and neither decadent nor intellectual. In fact, they were not Irish; they were Celts. Their homeland was what Europe had been before the Romans conquered it—a place innocent of complex political, economic, and military structures, inhabited by a fierce, imaginative, poetic tribe. At this point, faced with this precipitous revision of white European history, the Irish, who had shown a marked inclination toward

Seamus Deane

this view of themselves, finally took possession of the stereotype, modified the Celt into the Gael, and began that new interpretation of themselves known as the Irish literary revival. The revival, like the rebellion and the War of Independence, the treaty of 1922 (which partitioned Ireland into its present form), and the subsequent civil war, were simultaneously causes and consequences of the concerted effort to renovate the idea of the national character and of the national destiny. It was only when the Celt was seen by the English as a necessary supplement to their national character that the Irish were able to extend the idea of supplementarity to that of radical difference. This is a classic case of how nationalism can be produced by the forces that suppress it and can, at that juncture, mobilize itself into a form of liberation.

Such liberation as was achieved—and it was considerable—necessarily had its limits. It was a liberation into a specifically Irish, not a specifically human, identity. Since 1922, the developments in the South (now the Republic of Ireland) have emphasized this aspect of things. The Catholic church has successfully emphasized the uniqueness of the Irish Catholic tradition, seeing its role as the defender of a pious and chaste race in a degenerate and promiscuous world. Yeats too, especially in his later poetry, also wished to bestow upon his culture a unique role in helping humankind to survive the onslaught of the "filthy modern tide." In other words, Irish freedom declined into the freedom to become Irish in predestined ways. In that deep sense, the revolutionary impulse of the early part of the century was aborted. Now we have begun to come full circle again, repudiating that nationalist revolution, wishing—in some quarters—that 1916 had never happened and rewriting our history to cast doubt on the reality and the scandal of colonialism. Weary of the misconstrued Irish identity and understandably skeptical or derisive of the notion of Ireland's unique destiny, the Republic has surrendered the notion of identity altogether as a monotonous and barren anachronism and rushed to embrace all of those corporate, "international" opportunities offered by the European Economic Community and the tax-free visitations of international cartels.

It was then, in the midst of this process, that the North began its internecine conflict. This restored to center stage all those issues of communal identity, colonial interference, sectarianism, and racial stereotyping that had apparently been sidelined. It is at this juncture that Field Day positions itself.

The enterprise is threefold. It comprises theater, the Field Day pamphlets, and *The Field Day Anthology*. By 1990, Field Day will have completed the first phase of its operations. In the pamphlets, the general trend has been to analyze the various rhetorics of coercion and liberation that are so evident in modern Irish literature (particularly in Yeats and Joyce), in modern Irish political and legal discourse and practice, as well as in the systems of interpretation that have mediated these. As pamphlets, their nature and purpose require that they address these topics with some force and brevity in relation to the present northern or Anglo-Irish situation. In the theater, the central preoccupation has been with a particular experience of what we may call translation. By this I mean the adaptations, readjustments, and reorientations that are required of individuals and groups who have undergone a traumatic cultural and political crisis so fundamental that they must forge for themselves a new speech, a new history or life story that would give it some rational or coherent form. Brian Friels's plays, *Translations* (1980) and *Making History* (1988), Thomas Kilroy's *Double Cross* (1987), and Tom Paulin's adaptation of *Antigone* under the title *The Riot Act* (1985) are some of the most effective examples of the explorations characteristic of Field Day's theater. In all of them, a political crisis produces a clash of loyalties that is analyzable but irresolvable. In all three cases, the dramatic analysis centers on anxieties of naming, speaking, and voice and the relation of these to place, identity, and self-realiza-

Seamus Deane

tion. The plays and the pamphlets are intimately related as parts of a single project although they of course employ entirely different cadences in their development of the central discourse. *The Field Day Anthology of Irish Writing*, covering a span of 1,500 years, derives from these other activities. It is an act of repossession, resuming into the space of three massive volumes a selection of Irish literary, political, economic, philosophical, and other writings and presenting it, with a degree of ironic self-consciousness, as an integral and unitary "tradition" or amalgam of traditions. The point is not to establish a canon as such; it is to engage in the action of establishing a system that has an enabling, a mobilizing energy, the energy of assertion and difference, while remaining aware that all such systems—like anthologies of other national literatures—are fictions that have inscribed within them principles of hierarchy and of exclusion, as well as inclusion, that become evident only when the mass of material is organized into a particular form. It is not merely an exercise in regaining Swift, Berkeley, Goldsmith, Burke, Shaw, Yeats, Joyce, Beckett, and so forth from the neighboring fiction of English or British literature or literary tradition. It is a recuperation of these writers into the so-called other context, the inside reading of them in relation to other Irish writing, in order to modify and perhaps even distress other "outside" readings that have been unaware of that context and its force.

These three enterprises clearly involve a number of general questions, but they are addressed to a particular and tragic situation. The major communities in the North, Protestant and Catholic, unionist and nationalist, are compelled by the force of circumstances, some of which I have already mentioned, to rehearse positions from which there is no exit. Both communities have felt in the past and now do feel that the principles to which they are loyal are in grievous danger of being betrayed (or have already been betrayed) by those governments, in London and in Dublin, who were ostensibly their custodians. Each community feels that it is obliged, in the isolation subsequent to that betrayal, to retain the true faith, whether the faith of Irish republican nationalism, or of Protestant and British liberty. Each community sees the other as a threat to its existence. Each regards itself as, at one and the same time, the preserver of basic principle, caricatured by its erstwhile allies and friends into a blind and benighted tribe. Both communities are trapped within a tight geographic space, within a stifling set of stereotypes, half-persuaded that they are an embarrassment to the nation-states that cooperate to govern them. Even the usual vocabulary of democratic discourse fails to operate successfully. The Catholics are a minority in Northern Ireland but a majority in the island as a whole; they claim that their minority status was designed by the drawing of the border to perpetuate a Protestant majority. The Protestants are a majority in Northern Ireland and a minority in the whole island; they are also on occasion reminded that they are a minority within the United Kingdom. The structural similarities of their positions, their vacillation between feeling themselves a threatened minority or a powerful majority, their powerlessness in changing the situation and their power to sustain it, their demonizing of one another as a people natively given to violence, bigotry, and prejudice all combine with economic frailty to produce the sectarian dynamic. The much-vaunted British legal system has shown itself, both in Britain (when Irish people are involved) and in Ireland, to be nothing more than a system of political repression, because it too cannot afford to distinguish between the idea of the person as such and the idea of the person who can be understood to be such within the terms of the prevailing British ideology. In a crisis like this, the process of legitimation has a hard time of it; the scandalous corruption of law in Northern Ireland has made it clear that law is a matter of control, not of justice. This is in itself no stunning revelation; no colony or ex-colony needs to be reminded of it. But, like the bitter heritage of sectarianism, it shows that there is no basis for believing that the human being as such exists above and beyond the discriminations and categorizations that politics produce. A sectarian society kills people because they are Catholic or Protestant, republican, nationalist, unionist, terrorist, member of the security forces, or whatever. These distinctions are themselves the product of the very idea of society itself; they simply become more emphatic and crucial when the society's legitimation procedures are questioned.

Field Day, therefore, addresses this issue. A society needs a system of legitimation and, in seeking for it, always looks to a point of origin from which it can derive itself and its practices. That origin may be a document like the 1916 Proclamation of the Irish Republic, it may be Magna Carta, the Scottish Covenant, the revolution of 1688, 1789, or 1917. The Irish Revival and its predecessors had the right idea in looking to some legendary past for the legitimating origin of Irish society as one distinct from the British, which had a different conception of origin. But the search for origin, like that for identity, is self-contradictory. Once the origin is understood to be an invention, however necessary, it can never again be thought of as something "natural." A culture brings itself into being by an act of cultural invention that itself depends on an anterior legitimating nature. This is not merely a paradoxical game whereby the answer to "what came first?" is uselessly answered by "whatever came second." Nature may be a cultural invention, but it is nonetheless powerful for that. It is culture's most precious invention. In Northern Ireland that invention is not lost; it is in dispute. The terms of the dispute can be crude. The "native" Irish can say they came first; the Protestant planters can say that they were the first to create a civil society. These are not nugatory distinctions, for it is from them that so much of the later history of strife and disagreement evolves. Priority is a claim to power.

That is the reason for Field Day's preoccupation with naming, evident in the first three pamphlets by Tom Paulin, Seamus Heaney, and myself and evident too in the plays by

Brian Friel, Thomas Kilroy, and Tom Paulin to which I referred earlier. The naming or renaming of a place, the naming or renaming of a race, a region, a person, is, like all acts of primordial nomination, an act of possession. *The Field Day Anthology* is also an exercise in renaming, the resituation of many tests, well known and scarcely known, in a renovated landscape or context. All the various names for Ireland and for the Irish connection with Great Britain are themselves indications of the uncertainty, the failure of self-possession, which has characterized the various relationships and conditions to which the names refer. A selection of them would include Ireland, Eire, the Free State, the Republic of Ireland, the Twenty-Six Counties, the Six Counties, Ulster, Northern Ireland, the United Kingdom of Great Britain and Ireland, the United Kingdom of Great Britain and Northern Ireland. In a similar manner, one can point to the attempts to nominate literature in Ireland in its various forms; it is Irish Literature, Gaelic literature, Anglo-Irish literature, Irish literature in English, and so on. There are also Irish English, Hiberno-English, and Anglo-Irish as variations on the English spoken in Ireland. The multiplicity of these names is, of course, no bad thing in itself. They all refer to distinct and important differences of emphasis, meaning, interpretation. But their vigor conceals a corresponding weakness. That for which there is no all-embracing name cannot be comprehensively possessed. Instead of possession, we have various modes of sectarian appropriation.

In that respect, Northern Ireland enacts for us the more general crisis in which that which is an integral part of our history has become alien to us and known only to a subgroup or groups within the polity. The bulk of the Irish people are ignorant of and alien to the Irish language and its ancient literature; northern Protestants are alien to both that and to their own complex earlier history in Ireland. To remove ourselves from that condition into one in which all these lesions and occlusions are forgotten, in which the postmodernist simulacrum of pluralism supplants the

Seamus Deane

search for a legitimating mode of nomination and origin, is surely to pass from one kind of colonizing experience into another. For such pluralism refuses the idea of naming; it plays with diversity and makes a mystique of it; it is the concealed imperialism of the multinational, the infinite compatibility of all cultures with one another envisaged in terms of the ultimate capacity of all computers to read one another.

The three essays gathered here need only the briefest of introductions, since they speak so eloquently for themselves. They are the fifth in the series (each series comprising three essays), but they are the first in which the writers are not Irish. In each case, they have extended the range of Field Day's inquiry, giving it a purchase on issues—feminism, decolonization, and modernism—that it has so far lacked. It is part of our aim to continue this extension of our project so that it may provide illumination for problems that belong to other groups and regions and yet have a bearing on the current Irish situation. It may be doubted that we will find three more outstanding essayists than Terry Eagleton, Fredric Jameson, and Edward W. Said to enlarge and enrich our inquiry. I would like to register the gratitude of Field Day to all three and to the University of Minnesota Press for making this republication of the original pamphlets available to an American audience.

NATIONALISM:
IRONY AND
COMMITMENT

NATIONALISM: IRONY AND COMMITMENT

TERRY EAGLETON

"**N**ationalism," remarks an African character in Raymond Williams's novel *Second Generation* (London, 1964), "is in this sense like class. To have it, and to feel it, is the only way to end it. If you fail to claim it, or give it up too soon, you will merely be cheated, by other classes and other nations." Nationalism, like class, would thus seem to involve an impossible irony. It is sometimes forgotten that social class, for Karl Marx at least, is itself a form of alienation, canceling the particularity of an individual life into collective anonymity. Where Marx differs from the commonplace liberal view of such matters is in his belief that to undo this alienation you had to go, not around class, but somehow all the way through it and out the other side. To wish class or nation away, to seek to live sheer irreducible difference *now* in the manner of some contemporary poststructuralist theory, is to play straight into the hands of the oppressor. In a similar way, the philosopher Julia Kristeva has argued that the whole concept of gender is "metaphysical"—a violent stabilizing of the sheer precariousness and ambiguity of sexual identity to some spuriously self-identical essence.[1] The goal of a feminist politics would therefore be not an affirmation of some "female identity," but a troubling and subverting of all such sexual straitjacketing. Yet the grim truth remains that women are oppressed *as women*—that such sexual categories, ontologically empty though they may be, continue to exert an implacable political force. It would thus be the worst form of premature utopianism for women to strive now merely to circumvent their sexual identities, celebrating only the particular and polymorphous, rather than—once again—try somehow to go right through those estranging definitions to emerge somewhere on the other side. Women are not so much fighting for the freedom to be women—as though we all understood exactly what that meant—as for the freedom to be fully human; but that inevitably abstract humanity can be articulated in the here and now only through their womanhood, since this is the place where their humanity is wounded and refused. Sexual politics, like class or nationalist struggle, will thus necessarily be caught up in the very metaphysical categories it hopes finally to abolish; and any such movement will demand a difficult, perhaps ultimately impossible double optic, at once fighting on a terrain already mapped out by its antagonists and seeking even now to prefigure within that mundane strategy styles of being and identity for which we have as yet no proper names.

If the binary opposition between "man" and "woman" can always be deconstructed—if each term can always be shown to inhere parasitically within the other—then just the same is true of the opposition between those other virulently metaphysical forms of identity, Catholic and Protestant. Catholic, of course, means universal; so there is something curious in using it to define a particular kind of national identity. There is a good Joycean irony involved in establishing one's Irish identity by reference to a European capital. But the claim of the Roman Catholic church to universality is in any case only necessary once that status has been challenged by Protestantism, and so is no sooner raised than refuted, denying itself in the very act of assertion. Protestantism, on the other hand, is in one sense an aberration from such universal identity, an affirmation of national difference; yet it takes the historical form of a return to the pure universal essence of Christianity which the Church of Rome has supposedly contaminated. This heretical deviancy is thus more orthodox than orthodoxy itself, the very metaphysical truth or essence of that which it denounces. Catholicism itself already contains a certain Protestantism—*ecclesia semper reformanda*—without which constant deviating from itself it would not be truly itself; and Protestantism cannot exist as such without its historical antagonist. All that remains is now to explain this on the Falls and Shankill roads. Even those who had the insolence to do so would no doubt soon be brought to realize that their assertion of the metaphysical emptiness of Catholic and Protestant identities was itself metaphysically empty.

What one might call the "subjunctive mood" of "bad" or premature utopianism grabs instantly for a future, projecting itself by an act of will or imagination beyond the compromised political structures of the present. By failing to attend to those forces or fault lines *within* the present that, developed or prised open in particular ways, might induce that condition to surpass itself into a future, such utopianism is in danger of persuading us to desire uselessly rather than feasibly, and so, like the neurotic, to fall ill of unstaunchable longing. A desirable but unfeasible future, one that fails to found itself in the present in order to bridge us beyond it, is in this sense the reverse of the future offered us by some brands of social determinism, which is inevitable but not thereby necessarily desirable. (The inevitable, indeed, is usually pretty unpleasant.) A utopian thought that does not risk simply making us ill is one able to trace within the present that secret lack of identity with itself which is the spot where a feasible future might germinate—the place where the future overshadows and hollows out the present's spurious repleteness. To "know the future" can only mean to grasp the present under the sign of its internal contraditions, in the alienations of its desire, in its persistent inability ever quite to coincide with itself.

Just as the pious Jews, so Walter Benjamin reminds us,[2] were forbidden on pain of idolatry to fashion graven images of the God of the future, so political radicals are prohibited under pain of fetishism from blueprinting their ultimate desire. Marx himself, who began his political career in contention with the "wouldn't it be nice if" kind of revolutionary, is symptomatically silent for the most part about what a desirable future would look like, since the task of socialism is simply to identify and unlock those contradictions that are currently impeding its construction. The true soothsayers and clairvoyants are the technical experts hired by international capitalism to peer into the entrails of the system and assure its rulers that their profits are safe for another twenty years. Socialism belongs to the capitalist epoch as much as does the stock exchange, and like any emancipatory theory is preoccupied with putting itself progressively out of business. Emancipatory politics exist to bring about the material conditions that will spell their own demise, and so always have some peculiar self-destruct device built into them. If there are still political radicals on the scene in ten years' time, it will be a grim prospect. There will be no temple in the New Jerusalem, so the New Testament informs us, since ecclesial apparatuses belong to a history in conflict, not to the realm of freedom beyond that history's extreme horizon. All oppositional politics thus move under the sign of irony, knowing themselves ineluctably parasitic on their antagonists. Our grudge against the ruling order is not only that it has oppressed us in our social, sexual, or racial identities, but that it has thereby forced us to lavish an extraordinary amount of attention on these things, which are not in the long run all that important. Those of us who happen to be British, yet who object to what has been done historically to other peoples in our name, would far prefer a situation in which we could take being British for granted and think about something more interesting for a change.

Terry Eagleton

When Michel Foucault scathingly remarks that Marxism belongs entirely to the nineteenth century, the only bemusement for a Marxist is why he should assume that this constitutes a *criticism* of the creed. For the past is of course what we are made of; and the impasse of any transformative politics is that it can unravel what Marx and Stephen Dedalus call the nightmare of history only with the poor, contaminated instruments which that history has handed it. If Marxism belongs in a way to the museum, it is because capitalism has not yet awakened to its own drearily anachronistic nature, to the fact that it has long overstayed its welcome. Unable to remember the past, capitalism is bound compulsively to repeat it in that ceaseless sameness-within-difference that is commodity exchange; whereas for Marx the only truly memorable or historic event would be that by which we were able to leap from what he terms "prehistory"—the eternal recurrence of new variants on persistent forms of exploitation—to "history" proper: the kingdom of use value, sensuous particularity, and an endless productivity of difference. But all of that—what Marx enigmatically calls in *The Eighteenth Brumaire of Louis Bonaparte* "the poetry of the future"—is a content that, as he says, "goes beyond the phrase" of the present, and so can be figured only in silence, exile, and cunning. It is necessary, even so, to "remember" that future, about which nothing very positive can be said, in order to remember that as political radicals our identity stands and falls with those we oppose. It is in this sense, above all, that they have the upper hand.

Nationalism, Irish or otherwise, has never been particularly notable for its self-irony. Michael Collins never looked much like a man intent on doing himself out of business, a task that as it happened was left to others. And though irony may be a favored trope of the literary intellectual, it is hard to summon much of it when you have been blinded by a British army rubber bullet. How is such irony not simply to defuse our anger? It is hard for us today to reinvent the boldness with which a Leon Trotsky could polemicize against the whole concept of "proletarian culture" in his *Literature and Revolution*, since for Trotsky the proletariat was no more than a point of transition to a fully classless society. For Trotsky, the *proletkultists* have forgotten that social class, like colonialism, is a *relation*, and that a class or nation cannot live on as some corporate self-identical entity once those political relations have been dismantled. The whole concept of a "nationalist culture" must surely fall under a similar political judgment; yet if Trotsky could speak out on such a topic it was of course because he had won his authority to be heard, as architect of the Red Army and veteran of Bolshevik class struggle. He had, that is to say, been right the way through and come out somewhere on the other side—which could hardly be said of those who would now dismiss the notion of an Irish nationalist culture from the tap rooms of Tottenham or the senior common rooms of Oxbridge. Besides, Trotsky's negative assessment of a proletarian culture is not easily dissociable from his chronically oversanguine political temperament; and the whole concept, like that of a nationalist culture, is arguably too multiple and ambiguous in meaning to be simply spurned or celebrated.

The metaphysics of nationalism speak of the entry into full self-realization of a unitary subject known as the people. As with all such philosophies of the subject from Hegel to the present, this monadic subject must somehow curiously preexist its own process of materialization—must be equipped, even now, with certain highly determinate needs and desires, on the model of the autonomous human personality.[3] The problem is not so much one of discriminating among this subject's needs and desires—of determining, for example, which of them foreshadow a desirable future and which are merely the reflexes of an oppressive present—but rather the sheer fact that these desires are repressed. The model, in other words, is an expression/blockage one, of a familiar Romantic kind; and as with any

Terry Eagleton

model of such historical tenacity there is undoubtedly much to be said for it. Subjects, national or otherwise, do indeed experience needs that are repressed but demand realization; it is just that one ironic effect of such repression is to render us radically uncertain of what our needs really are. The very repressive conditions that make it necessary for the subject to express itself freely also tend to render it partially opaque to itself. If subjects have needs, then we already know what one at least of these needs must be, namely, the need to know what one's needs are. The metaphysics of nationalism tend to obscure this point, by assuming a subject somehow intuitively present to itself; in privileging the concept of self-realization, it elevates a subject-object relation over a subject-subject one, forgetting that the expression and formulation of needs are always a dialogical affair, that needs and desires are always in some sense received back from an "other." On the other hand, those contemporary thinkers, like Jürgen Habermas, who recall us to this truth tend to forget in their turn about the political necessities of lifting the repression, so that such dialogism can actually take place. A radical politics can prescribe what must be done for this to occur; but it cannot prescribe the content of what will then be lived, for the content, as Marx says, goes beyond the phrase. All radical politics are thus in a profound sense formalistic. As long as we can now adequately describe the transformations our political actions intend, we have failed by that token to advance beyond reformism.

If women are oppressed as women, are the Irish oppressed as Irish? In one sense, surely not: it was never of much interest to British imperialism whether the Irish were Irish or Eskimo, white or black, whether they worshiped tree gods or the Trinity. It is not their ethnic peculiarity but their territory and labor power that have entranced the British. The Irish are simply denizens of a convenient neighboring island; as long as they are *other* than the British they do not, like women, require certain specific innate characteristics to be ruled over. (The oppression of women is not of course reducible to such innate characteristics, but it is not independent of them either.) In another sense, however, it is clearly abstract caviling to maintain that the Irish people has not been oppressed *as* Irish. However fundamentally indifferent colonialism may be to the nature of the peoples it does down, the fact remains that a particular people is in effect done down *as such*. And it is this fact that the truth of nationalism illuminates. As with the case of women, then, to attempt to bypass the specificity of one's identity in the name of freedom will always be perilously abstract, even once one has recognized that such an identity is as much a construct of the oppressor as one's "authentic" sense of oneself. Any emancipatory politics must begin with the specific, then, but must in the same gesture leave it behind. For the freedom in question is not the freedom to "be Irish" or "be a woman," whatever that might mean, but simply the freedom now enjoyed by certain other groups to determine their identity as they may wish. Ironically, then, a politics of difference or specificity is in the first place in the cause of sameness and universal identity—the right of a group victimized in its particularity to be on equal terms with others as far as their self-determination is concerned. This is the kernel of truth of bourgeois Enlightenment: the abstract universal right of all to be free, the shared essence or identity of all human subjects to be autonomous. In a further dialectical twist, however, this truth itself must be left behind as soon as seized; for the only point of enjoying such universal abstract equality is to discover and live one's own particular difference. The *telos* of the entire process is not, as the Enlightenment believed, universal truth, right and identity, but concrete particularity. It is just that such particularity has to pass through that abstract equality and come out somewhere on the other side, somewhere quite different from where it happens to be standing now. The most sterile form of nationalism, to continue the Hegelian idiom, is one that merely elevates a "bad" or given particularity to the universal. The release of concrete, sensuously particular use value—to put the matter in Marxist terms—cannot come about by circumventing the abstract universal equalizations of exchange value, but only, somehow, by entering into that alienated logic in order to turn it against itself. As Oscar Wilde well understood, socialism is essential for genuine individualism; and if Wilde's own outrageous individualism prefigures that in one sense, it also testifies in its very flamboyant artifice to the way in which any individualism of the present is bound to be a strained, fictive, parodic travesty of the real thing.

It is part of the embarrassment of bourgeois ideology that it has never really been able to reconcile difference and identity, the particular and the universal, and this for excellent historical reasons. The sensuous particularity of human needs and desires belongs in classical bourgeois thought to the degraded sphere of "civil society," the essentially private realms of family and economic production. The ethical and political spheres, by contrast, are where men and women encounter one another as abstractly equalized universal subjects. And one of the tasks of bourgeois ideology is to square the grotesque discrepancy between these two worlds as brazenly as it can. The most effective critique of bourgeois society is accordingly one that like Marxism is "immanent," installing itself within the very logic of that order's own most cherished values in order to unmask the necessary disconnection of this ideal universal realm from the sordidly particularistic appetites it serves to mystify. Other kinds of radical critique are also possible, however, that seize upon one pole of this particular/universal opposition in order to turn it against the other. In the manner of Enlightenment radicalism, you can press for the revolutionary *extension* of universal rights, embarrassing such ideals by reminding them forcibly of the groups and peoples they exclude; or, like Romantic radicalism, you can embrace the local, sensuously specific, and irreducibly individual and seek to shipwreck an abstract idealism on the rock of the concretely real. These strategies are not actually as antithetical as they seem, since nothing could be more abstract than so-called Romantic "immediacy"; but they constitute between them a kind of pincer movement to aggravate the contradictions of the bourgeois social order.

If Enlightenment radical means, in the context of Ireland, Wolfe Tone and the United Irishmen, the pieties of sensuous particularity mean the aestheticized politics of Young Ireland and much that has flowed from them. Particularity is either suppressed in the totality of universal Reason, the concrete Irish subject sublated to a citizen of the world, or celebrated as a unique, irreducible state of being impenetrable to all alien Enlightenment rationality. In modern European thought, however, the "aesthetic" signifies less sensuous particularity in itself, than the very ideological model of how this contradiction between specific and universal may be harmoniously resolved. The work of art is itself governed by a total law, but a law that appears mysteriously, spontaneously at one with the very self-determining autonomy of each of its component parts. Behind this aesthetic model stands a new kind of bourgeois polity, in which—since the centralized law of feudal absolutism has been overthrown—each individual must somehow give the law to himself, work all by herself, discover the law inscribed in her very affections, sensations, and bodily impulses. What is in question here, in short, is that historically new form of power that Antonio Gramsci has termed "hegemony"—that process whereby the particular subject so introjects a universal law as to consent to its imperatives in the form of consenting to his own deepest being.

Any such hegemony is far more difficult to construct in colonial conditions. For the law in such conditions will appear visibly alien, heteronomous to the individual rather than the secret inner structure of her identity. It is the embarrassment of colonial ruling classes, as it is not so much of the metropolitan governing elites, that they figure as perceptibly "other" to their subordinates, perhaps speaking a foreign language or having a different color of skin. The law of political power always works best when it is invisible, as Edmund Burke well understood; for the law to be salient is for it to risk becoming itself an object of contestation. It is therefore perhaps not surprising that in Ireland the "aesthetic" as totalizing solution to the conflict of universal and particular is rather less in evidence. Instead, the aesthetic tends to emerge as one side of the dilemma—as expressive of the lived specificity of a unique people in the teeth of that abstract universalism that is taken to be the very mark of modernity. This is not to say, on the other hand, that the aesthetic as "disinterested" mythic solution to real contradictions is not in evidence in Ireland at all. There are Irish critics and commentators who deploy the term today as a privileged mark of that decency, civility, and cultivation of which an uncouth nationalism is fatally bereft. In the stalest of Arnoldian clichés, the poetic is still being counterposed to the political—which is only to say that the "poetic" as we have it today was, among other things, historically constructed to carry out just that business of suppressing political conflict. Imagination and enlightened liberal reason are still being offered to us in Ireland today as the antithesis of sectarianism; and like all such idealized values they forget their own roots in a social class and history not unnoted for its own virulent sectarianism, then and now. This bankrupt Irish Arnoldianism is particularly ironic when one considers that the title of Arnold's own major work, *Culture and Anarchy*, might well have been rewritten as *Britain and Ireland*. The liberal humanist notion of Culture was constituted, among other things, to marginalize such peoples as the Irish, so that it is particularly intriguing to find this sectarian gesture being rehearsed by a few of the Irish themselves.

If the rift between sensuous particularity and idealist abstraction has proved a constant source of unease for bourgeois society, it has proved something of the same for that society's political antagonists. For it is hard to see how the left can simply "dialectically mediate" such oppositions without merely rehearsing the mystificatory gestures of the right. Somewhere around the turn of the nineteenth century, the left fatally surrendered the aesthetic to the right. Tom Paine's plain-minded scoffing at Burke's extravagantly metaphorical diction, or Mary Wollstonecraft's scathing dismissal of his "pampered sensibility," are cases in point. Feeling, imagination, the priority of local affections and unarguable allegiances, a subliminally nurturing cultural tradition: these things, from Burke and Coleridge to Yeats and T. S. Eliot, are effectively confiscated by political reaction, which is shrewd enough not to attempt to rule by the naked light of reason or utility alone. The political left is then doubly disabled: if it seeks to evolve its own discourse of place, body, inheritance, sensuous need, it will find itself miming the cultural forms of its opponents; if it does not do so it will appear bereft of a body, marooned with a purely rationalist politics that has cut loose from the intimate affective depths of the poetic. The feminist analogy is exact: if women speak the discourse of the body, the unconscious, the dark underside of formal speech—in a word, the Gothic— they merely confirm their aberrant status; if they appropriate like Wollstonecraft the language of radical rationalism, they are no different from men. Left political theory in Europe today is consequently divided between the rationalism of a Habermas, with his "ideal speech communities" of universal, abstractly equal subjects from whom all bodily inclination has been drained, and the anarchic particularism of the poststructuralists, with their heady celebrations of delirium, pure difference, the fragment, flashes of libidinal intensity, against a rational totality now denounced as brutally totalitarian.

I have suggested that the aesthetic as a totalization of particular and universal is in general absent in Ireland; but then what else, you might claim, is *Ulysses*? Where could one discover a more triumphant unity of the two than in that text, in which every particular opens cunningly out into the cosmic, every time, place, or identity is secretly pregnant with every other? The aesthetics of *Ulysses* are in this sense pretty standard Hegelian stuff, and among other things fit compensation for the pains of exile. If anywhere is everywhere, then you can scribble away in Trieste without ever having left Dublin. But it would surely be obtuse to overlook the enormous irony with which the novel manages this remorseless totalization, which gestures to its own flagrant arbitrariness in its very poker-faced exhaustiveness. The form of *Ulysses* is indeed in one sense an aesthetic resolution of historical contradictions — not least of the conflict between the new international circuits of capitalism, with their correlative cosmopolitan centers of culture in Paris, London, Berlin, and New York, and the older national formations or cultural traditions that are being increasingly outmoded. Modernism is at once, contradictorily, an exhilarating estrangement of such clapped-out national lineages from the powerfully distancing perspectives of exiles, and an expression of the rootless conditions of an international monopoly capitalism, whose abstractly universalist forms are mimed by modernism's own progressively abstract techniques.[4] If, like Joyce, you have little enough of a rich national lineage to begin with, then you become paradigmatic in your very colonial dispossession of the destiny of even advanced national formations in the era of international capital. For entirely different reasons, neither colonial backwardness nor the inbred provincialism of the imperial nations can produce the art that the age demands. Since Ireland, from the standpoint of the advanced societies, is already a kind of nonplace and nonidentity, it can lend itself peculiarly well to a cosmopolitan modernism for which all places and identities are becoming progressively interchangeable.

If *Ulysses* "resolves" contradictions, however, the sweated Flaubertian labor with which this is accomplished points to the effective impossibility of the whole project. The textual totality that lends a particular time and place fresh centrality does so in order to betray simultaneously just how radically contingent any such place or time has now become. Joyce's compliment to Ireland, in inscribing it on the cosmopolitan map, is in this sense distinctly backhanded. The novel celebrates and undermines the Irish national formation at a stroke, deploying the full battery of cosmopolitan modernist techniques to re-create it while suggesting with its every breath just how easily it could have done the same for Bradford or the Bronx. Something of the same ambiguity haunts *Finnegans Wake*, a work that, as its radical apologists have pointed out, confounds and commingles all distinct identities in a manner scandalous to the rigorous hierarchies of orthodox bourgeois culture. Yet it is not only that this free play of difference and desire is arguably still contained within a *Ulysses*-like structure of eternal recurrence—that what you lose on the semiotic swings you make up on the Viconian roundabouts. It is also that what is turned disruptively against bourgeois *culture* is in a sense bourgeois *economy*: the leveling, equalizing, indifferent operations of the commodity form itself, which respects no unique identity, transgresses all frontiers, melts solidity into air, and profanes the holy. The *Wake*'s anarchic differencing is possible only on the basis of a secret homogenizing of reality, a prior equalizing of all items that then enables them to enter into the most shockingly idiosyncratic permutations.[5] There comes a point, as Hegel was well aware, at which "pure" difference merely collapses back into "pure" identity, united as they are in their utter indeterminacy.

Joyce, then, poses the problem of totalization, rather than providing us with any very adequate solution. The ironic overtotalization of *Ulysses* is a pedantic travesty of modern European aesthetics, whereas the *Wake* displays an enormous, disabling distance between its abstract "deep structure" and its textual particulars. Either way, dialectical mediation is disrupted: immediate and universal are either too comically close for comfort or riven apart. Such ironic, impossible, or aporetic relations between the two are perhaps still necessarily the case today, in the relations between particular political struggles and the goal of universal emancipation. What any oppressed group has most vitally in common is just the shared fact of their oppression. Their collective identity is in this sense importantly negative, defined less by shared positive characteristics than by a common antagonism to some political order. That negative collective identity, however, is bound over a period of time to generate a positive particular culture, without which political emancipation is probably impossible. Nobody can live in perpetual deferment of their sense of selfhood, or free themselves from bondage without a strongly affirmative consciousness of who they are. Without such self-consciousness, one would not even know what one lacked; and a subject that thinks itself complete feels no need to revolt. In this sense, the "negativity" of an oppressed people—its sense of itself as dislocated and depleted—already implies a more positive style of being. The true triumph of alienation would be not to know that one was alienated at all. But since any such positive identity evolves *within* oppressive conditions, partly as compensatory for them, it can never be an unambiguous political gain, and will always be to some extent collusive with its antagonists. The paradox or aporia of any transformative politics is that it demands, to be successful, a "centered," resolute, self-confident agent, but would not be necessary in the first place if such self-confidence were genuinely possible. Radical change is thus rendered highly vulnerable by what makes it necessary in the first place. The ideal revolutionary subject has broken with an imposed political identity into a kind of nameless, subversive negativity, yet has a sense of his or her own autonomous powers and capacities that far outstrips the hazy, indeterminate awareness of ourselves as agents that we derive from routine social life. This is not the kind of conundrum that any discourse of dialectical mediation will readily clarify.

Where human subjects politically begin, in all their sensuous specificity, is with certain needs and desires. Yet need and desire are also what render us nonidentical with ourselves, opening us up to some broader social dimension; and what is posed within this dimension is the question of what *general* conditions would be necessary for our particular needs and desires to be fulfilled. Mediated through the general in this way, particular demands cease to be self-identical and return to themselves transformed by a discourse of the other. The feminist, nationalist, or trade unionist might now come to recognize that in the long run none of their desires is realizable without the fulfillment of the others'. Where the antidialecticians are right is that such a recognition cannot be *lived* as simple, seamless unity. Indeed, the fact that the Hegelian totality cannot be lived was Kierkegaard's recurrent complaint against it. It is only ambiguously, precariously, that any of us can experience at once the necessary absolutism of a particular demand—to be freed, for example, from an immediate, intolerable oppression—and the more general truth that no one such demand, however just and urgent, can finally exhaust or preprogram a political future in which the content will have gone beyond the phrase. As Kierkegaard might have said, it is a matter of trying to live that dialectic passionately, ironically, in all of its elusive impossibility, rather than merely providing an elegant theoretical formulation of it.

NOTES

1. See Julia Kristeva, "La femme, ce n'est jamais ça," *Tel Quel*, 59 (Autumn 1974).

2. See Walter Benjamin, "Theses on the Philosophy of History," in H. Arendt (ed.), *Illuminations* (London: Jonathan Cape, 1970), 266.

3. For a valuable critique of this ideology, see Seyla Benhabib, *Critique, Norm, and Utopia* (New York: Columbia University Press, 1986).

4. For an excellent account of modernism in these terms, see Raymond Williams, "Beyond Cambridge English," in *Writing in Society* (London: Verso, 1983).

5. "The pluralism of (Joyce's) styles and languages, the absorbent nature of his controlling myths and systems, finally gives a certain harmony to varied experience. But, it could be argued, it is the harmony of indifference,

one in which everything is a version of something else, where sameness rules over diversity, where contradiction is finally and disquietingly written out'' (Seamus Deane, *Heroic Styles: The Tradition of an Idea*, Field Day pamphlet no. 4 [Derry 1984], 16).

MODERNISM AND
IMPERIALISM

MODERNISM
AND IMPERIALISM

FREDRIC JAMESON

This is a time in which, at least in part owing to what is called postmodernism, there seems to be renewed interest in finding out what modernism really *was* (note the past tense), and in rethinking that now historical phenomenon in new ways, which are not those we have inherited from the participants and the players, the advocates and the practitioners themselves. But this has also been a time, over perhaps an even longer span of years, in which the matter of what imperialism *is* (note the tense) and how it functions has been a subject of intense debate and discussion among the theorists, and not only the economists, the historians, and the political scientists. A range of very complex theories and models indeed—probably more incomprehensible than most forms of contemporary literary theory—have come into being which any serious discussion of this issue has to acknowledge.

Any discussion of the relationship of modernism and imperialism will therefore generally require, not one, but two lengthy preambles, before it reaches its topic. It is, however, important to be clear in advance of what that topic is: it will not, in the present case, involve what can be called the literature of imperialism, since that literature (Kipling, Rider Haggard, Verne, Wells) is by and large not modernist in any formal sense, and, emerging from subcanonical genres like the adventure tale, remained "minor" or "marginal" during the hegemony of the modern and its ideology and values (even Conrad explicitly draws on more archaic storytelling forms).[1]

The hypothesis to be explored here is both more formalistic and more sweeping than the affirmation that imperialism as such produced its specific literature and left palpable traces on the *content* of other metropolitan[2] literary works of the period. I want in fact to suggest that the structure of imperialism also makes its mark on the inner forms and structures of that new mutation in literary and artistic language to which the term modernism is loosely applied. This last has of course multiple social determinants: any general theory of the modern—assuming one to be possible in the first place—would also wish to register the informing presence of a range of other historically novel phenomena: modernization and technology; commodity reification; monetary abstraction and its effects on the sign system; the social dialectic of reading publics; the emergence of mass culture; the embodiment of new forms of the psychic subject on the physical sensorium. Nor is the relative weight and importance of the emergence of a whole new global and imperial system in this constellation of "factors" at all clear, even in a speculative way. The present essay is limited to the isolation of this determinant alone, the presence of a new force, which cannot be reduced to any of those aforementioned.

However extrinsic and extraliterary the fact of imperialism may at first seem, there is at least a chronological justification for exploring its influence. If we take, as the codification of the new imperialist world system, the emblematic date of 1884—the year of the Berlin Conference, which parceled Africa out among the "advanced" powers—a whole range of literary and artistic events spring to mind which at the very least suggest analogous breaks and emergences: the death of Victor Hugo in the following year, for example, has often been seen as the inaugural moment of that whole new symbolist and Mallarmean aesthetic which his disappearance suddenly revealed to have already existed in full development behind his massive presence. The choice of such emblematic breaks is not an empirically verifiable matter but a historiographic decision; nor are chronological parallels of this kind much more at the outset than incentives to construct new and more complex and interesting historical narratives, whose usefulness cannot be predicted before the fact. But when, as we shall see, the parallel also seems to hold at the other end of such chronological series and the end of modernism to coincide with the restructuration of the classical imperialist world system, our curiosity as to possible interrelationships can surely only be sharpened, even if it has been restricted in another way.

For the emphasis on form and formal innovation and modification implies that our privileged texts and objects of study here will be those that scarcely evoke imperialism as such at all; that seem to have no specifically political content in the first place; that offer purely stylistic or linguistic peculiarities for analysis. One of the more commonly held stereotypes about the modern has of course in general been that of its apolitical character, its turn inward and away from the social materials associated with realism, its increased subjectification and introspective psychologization, and, not least, its aestheticism and its ideological commitment to the supreme value of a now autonomous Art as such. None of these characterizations strikes me as adequate or persuasive any longer; they are part of the baggage of an older modernist ideology which any contemporary theory of the modern will wish to scrutinize and to dismantle. But there is something to be said in the present context, for beginning with the formalist stereotype of the modern, if only to demonstrate with greater force the informing presence of the extraliterary, of the political and the economic within it.[3]

But such is not the only restriction on the present topic: it also involves some restrictions that concern its other term—imperialism as such, which must also now be delimited. I take it, for instance, that only those theories of imperialism which acknowledge the Marxist problematic (in however heretical or revisionist a fashion) are of concern here since it is only within that problematic that a coordination between political phenomena (violence, domination, control, state power) and economic phenomena (the market, investment, exploitation, underconsumption, crisis) is systematically pursued. Exclusively political theories of imperialism (such as Schumpeter's) slip not merely toward moralizing, but also toward metaphysical notions of human nature (the lust for power or domination), which end up dissolving the historical specificity of the thing itself and disperse the phenomenon of imperialism throughout human history, wherever bloody conquests are to be found (which is to say: everywhere!). At any rate, if it is the link between imperialism and modernism that is in question here (and between imperialism and *Western* modernism at that), then clearly imperialism must here mean the imperialist dynamic of capitalism proper, and not the wars of conquest of the various ancient empires.

But even in the case of Marxist theories of imperialism, a further historical qualification now needs to be set in place: namely, that the Marxist approach to imperialism is crucially modified and restructured in the mid-twentieth century.[4] People generally remember that Lenin wrote a very influential pamphlet on imperialism during World War I; they probably suspect anyone who uses this word "imperialism" too frequently of being a Marxist; and if they have had any greater exposure to these discussions, they know that the term has something to do with the problems of Third World societies and with underdevelopment, with the debt as well, with the IMF and American investments and bases abroad, with support for dictators and anxieties about Soviet influence, and perhaps only ultimately—in the last instance!—with marines and gunboat intervention or with a formal colonial structure. What must now be observed is that the term "imperialism" when used in the so-called Marxian classics—in Marx himself, in Lenin, in Hilferding and in Bukharin, with a certain exceptionality for the work of Rosa Luxemburg—has none of these connotations. For the most part, the older Marxist theorists of imperialism followed Marx himself (in the famous letters on India) in assuming that capitalist penetration would lead directly to positive economic development in what are now known as Third World countries. The very widely held contemporary belief—that, following the title of Walter Rodney's influential book, capitalism leads on the contrary to "the development of underdevelopment," and that imperialism systematically cripples the growth of its colonies and its dependent areas—this belief is utterly absent from what may be called the first moment of Marxist theories of imperialism and is indeed everywhere explicitly contradicted by them, where they raise the matter at all.[5] The point is, however, that they do not often raise the matter in that form for the good reason that during this period the word "imperialism" designates, not the relationship of metropolis to colony, but rather the rivalry of the various imperial and metropolitan nation-states among themselves. It becomes immediately clear, then, that we risk all kinds of historical confusions and anachronisms if we ignore this usage and transfer our own contemporary sense of the word to contexts in the modernist period.

For it is in our time, since World War II, that the problem of imperialism is as it were restructured: in the age of neocolonialism, of decolonization accompanied by the emergence of multinational capitalism and the great transnational corporations, it is less the rivalry of the metropolitan powers among each other that strikes the eye (our occasional problems with Japan, for example, do not project that impending World War-type conflict that nagged at the awareness of the *belle époque*); rather, contemporary theorists, from Paul

Baran on to the present day, have been concerned with the internal dynamics of the relationship between First and Third World countries, and in particular the way in which this relationship—which is now very precisely what the word "imperialism" means for us—is one of necessary subordination or dependency, and that of an economic type, rather than a primarily military one. This means that in the period from World War I to World War II the axis of otherness has as it were been displaced: it first governed the relationship of the various imperial subjects with each other; it now designates the relationship between a generalized imperial subject (most often the United States, but frequently enough also Britain or France and Japan, not to speak of those new kinds of metropolitan centers which are South Africa or Israel) and its various others or objects. That would be the historical way of putting it; but since (naturally enough) we think we have discovered some more basic truths about the dynamics of imperialism than our forefathers in Lenin's time, one could also describe the displacement this way: in that older period, from 1884 to World War I, the relationship of domination between First and Third World was masked and displaced by an overriding (and perhaps ideological) consciousness of imperialism as being essentially a relationship between First World powers or the holders of Empire, and this consciousness tended to repress the more basic axis of otherness, and to raise issues of colonial reality only incidentally.

Culturally, the causes as well as the effects of this shift can be rapidly evoked. We think about the Third World in a different way today, not merely because of decolonization and political independence, but above all because these enormously varied cultures all now speak in their own distinctive voices. Nor are those voices any longer marginal ones that we are free to overlook; at least one of them—Latin American literature, since the *boom*—has today become perhaps the principal player on the scene of world culture, and has had an unavoidable and inescapable influence, not merely

Fredric Jameson

on other Third World cultures as such, but on First World literature and culture as well. It would be easy to demonstrate a presence of other such voices in First World cultural situations outside the United States as well, as for example in Britain today. Meanwhile, it is significant that in the United States itself, we have come to think and to speak of the emergence of an *internal* Third World and of internal Third World voices, as in black women's literature or Chicano literature for example. When the other speaks, he or she becomes another subject, which must be consciously registered as a problem by the imperial or metropolitan subject—whence the turn of what are still largely Western theories of imperialism in a new direction, toward that other, and toward the structures of underdevelopment and dependency for which we are responsible.

But in the modernist period this is by no means the case. The prototypical paradigm of the Other in the late nineteenth century—in Zola's *La Débâcle* (1982), for example—is the other imperial nation-state: in this case, the Germans, who are the quintessential ogres and bogeymen of childhood nightmare, physically alien and terrifying, barbarous, uncivilized, and still not terribly remote, as stereotypes, from the archaic "wild man of the Middle Ages," who incarnates everything fascinating and frightening about the unbridled id for an agricultural or village society.[6] Such "others" will then circulate in paler and more respectable forms in high literature during this period—as in the various foreigners who add an exotic note to high society in the English novel (E. M. Forster's Germans, in *Howards End*, function to reverse this xenophobia in a kind of therapeutic liberal tolerance and self-critique); while the more radical otherness of colonized, non-Western peoples tends to find its representational place in that noncanonical adventure literature of imperialism to which we have already referred.

But this masking of one axis of otherness by a very different one, this substitution of rivalry for exploitation, and of a First World set of characters for a Third World presence, may be thought of as a strategy of representational containment, which scarcely alters the fundamental imperialist structure of colonial appropriation, or of what Jacques Berque has memorably called the "dépossession du monde" of the colonized peoples. Its effects are representational effects, which is to say a systematic block on any adequate consciousness of the structure of the imperial system: but these are just as clearly objective effects and will have their most obvious consequences in the aesthetic realm, where the mapping of the new imperial world system becomes impossible, since the colonized other who is its essential other component or opposite number has become invisible.

It is in this situation that modernist representation emerges, and this is indeed in general the relationship of formal and cultural change to what we have called its social "determinants," which present a radically altered situation (new raw materials of a social, psychological, or physical type) to which a fresh and unprecedented aesthetic response is demanded, generally by way of formal, structural, and linguistic invention.[7] But what the new situation of imperialism looks like from the standpoint of cultural or aesthetic production now needs to be characterized, and its seems best to do so by distinguishing its problems from those of an internal industrialization and commodification in the modernizing metropolis. This last seems most often (paradoxically) to have been lived in terms of a generalized loss of meaning, as though its subject measured the increase in human power negatively, by way of the waning of tradition and religious absolutes, at the same time that the fact of praxis and production was only too susceptible to distortion by and concealment beneath the reifying logic and of the commodity form.

What is determined by the colonial system is now a rather different kind of meaning loss than this one: for colonialism means that a significant structural segment of the economic system as a whole is now located elsewhere, beyond the metropolis, outside of the daily life and existential experi-

Fredric Jameson

ence of the home country, in colonies over the water whose own life experience and life world—very different from that of the imperial power—remain unknown and unimaginable for the subjects of the imperial power, whatever social class they may belong to. Such spatial disjunction has as its immediate consequence the inability to grasp the way the system functions as a whole. Unlike the classical stage of national or market capitalism, then, pieces of the puzzle are missing; it can never be fully reconstructed; no enlargement of personal experience (in the knowledge of other social classes, for example), no intensity of self-examination (in the form of whatever social guilt), no scientific deductions on the basis of the internal evidence of First World data, can ever be enough to include this radical otherness of colonial life, colonial suffering, and exploitation, let alone the structural connections between that and this, between absent space and daily life in the metropolis. To put it in other words, this last—daily life and existential experience in the metropolis—which is necessarily the very content of the national literature itself, can now no longer be grasped immanently; it no longer has its meaning, its deeper reason for being, within itself. As artistic content it will now henceforth always have something missing about it, but in the sense of a privation that can never be restored or made whole simply by adding back in the missing component: its lack is rather comparable to another dimension, an outside like the other face of a mirror, which it constitutively lacks, and which can never be made up or made good. This new and historically original problem in what is itself a new kind of content now constitutes the situation and the problem and the dilemma, the formal contradiction, that modernism seeks to solve; or better still, it is only that new kind of art which reflexively perceives this problem and lives this formal dilemma that can be called modernism in the first place.

Now of course one's simplest first thought, faced with this problem of a global space that like the fourth dimension somehow constitutively escapes you, is no doubt to make a map: nor is *Ulysses* by any means the first, let alone the only, literary work of the imperialist period that stakes its bet on the properties of maps. The very title of Conrad's *Heart of Darkness*, whatever other resonances it comes to have, is literally determined by the reference to cartography. But cartography is not the solution, but rather the problem, at least in its ideal epistemological form as social cognitive mapping on the global scale. The map, if there is to be one, must somehow emerge from the demands and constraints of the spatial perceptions of the individual; and since Britain is generally thought of as the quintessential imperialist power, it may be useful to begin with a sample of English spatial experience:

> The train sped northward, under innumerable tunnels. It was only an hour's journey, but Mrs. Munt had to raise and lower the window again and again. She passed through the South Welwyn Tunnel, of tragic fame. She traversed the immense viaduct, whose arches span untroubled meadows and the dreamy flow of Tewin Water. She skirted the parks of politicians. At times the Great North Road acompanied her, more suggestive of infinity than any railway awakening, after a nap of a hundred years, to such life as is conferred by the stench of motorcars, and to such culture as is implied by the advertisements of antibilious pills. To history, to tragedy, to the past, to the future, Mrs. Munt remained equally indifferent; hers but to concentrate on the end of her journey, and to rescue poor Helen from this dreadful mess.[8]

This episode, from the opening pages of *Howards End*, is characteristic of Forster's duplicities, and offers an amiable simplicity filled with traps and false leads. Pockets of philosophical complexity are hidden away beneath its surface, and they include reflections on nature and industrialization, on authentic and inauthentic existential time (Mrs. Munt's version of Heideggerian *Sorge*), and a firm but tactful consciousness of English class realities. The novel will then undertake to spell these out and to make sure that what the reader has been encouraged to overlook here becomes at length an unavoidable message, in terms of which we may then leaf back and gloss the present text in some detail. But it will remain a gloss on what is essentially a spatial representation and a spatial perception: the philosophical thoughts (which in any case involve space, as we shall see) will finally have been dependent on space, and inexpressible without it. This is of course a cinematographic kind of space, with its Einsteinian observer on a train moving through a landscape whose observation it alters at the very moment that it makes it possible. But what is most significant is not some possible influence of nascent cinema on Forster or on the modernist novel in general, but rather the confluence of the two distinct formal developments, of movie technology on the one hand, and of a certain type of modernist or protomodernist language on the other, both of which seem to offer some space, some third term, between the subject and the object alike. Cinematographic perception is in that sense neither subjective nor psychological: there is nothing private or personal about it (and it was for that reason that I suggested, above, that characterizations of the modern as some inward turn were misleading). But it is not objective either in any conventional sense of realism or empiricism: nothing is indeed quite so perverse or aberrant for the truly postmodern person as the polemic expression "photographic realism"—as though photography, today so mysterious and contradictory an experience, had anything reassuringly trustworthy or reliable about it, for us a most unlikely guarantor of verisimilitude! This is why, although the category of *style* remains a fundamental one of the various modernisms, emerging with them and disappearing again when the psychic subject is notoriously eclipsed in the postmodern moment, it seems urgent to disjoin it from conventional notions of psychology and subjectivity: whence the therapeutic usefulness of the cinematographic parallel, where an apparatus takes the place of human psychology and perception. But this can most effectively be achieved by recoordinating the concept of style with some new account of the experience of space, both together now marking the emergence of the modern as such, and the place from which a whole bewilderingly varied set of modernisms begins to flourish.

Forster, at best a closet modernist, may seem an unlikely enough illustration of this process; but it was its tendential emergence that interested us, and not the full-blown thing itself. Meanwhile, if it is argued that England, the very heartland of imperialism, is also that national terrain which seems to have been the least propitious for the development of any indigenous modernism,[9] then that is surely also relevant for our present topic.

Yet at least one moment in the present passage seems to hold all the possibilities of some properly modernist language, past and future, instinct within itself, from Baudelaire to Eliot: a figure which speeds by like Mrs. Munt's surroundings, only its false modesty drawing attention to itself (as always in Forster). It is "the Great North Road . . . suggestive of infinity." One sees what is meant, of course, and the reader dutifully recomposes some inner film around the visual properties of the highway, its great sweep and curve away from the train tracks; its empty endlessness, on which a few (multiple) vehicles reinforce the investment of the observer by a single massive conveyance; its desolation, finally, denuded and thereby closer to the Idea than the unavoidable contamination of the railway interior by a modernizing and commercial history. This is at least what the figure gives us to see; but, particularly when you come to know that Forster continues to use the word "infinity" as though it really means something, the meaning itself grows less and less evident. Or perhaps it might be better to characterize this moment of a properly modernist *style* as one in which an appearance of meaning is pressed into the service of the notation of a physical perception. In fact, the reading problem turns on the objective uncertainty as to the structure of this figure: it is undecidable whether the Great

Fredric Jameson

North Road is the tenor or the vehicle; whether the roadway is intended, as in analogous moments in Baudelaire, to concretize the nebulous metaphysical concept, "infinity," and by a momentary transfer of its visual properties to make that vague but lofty word a more vivid linguistic player in the textual game; or whether, on the other hand, it is rather the metaphysical prestige of the more noble Idea that is supposed to resonate back on the banal highway, lending it *numen* and thereby transforming it into the merest promise of expressivity without having to affirm it as some official "symbol" of the conventionally mendacious kind. Modernism is itself this very hesitation; it emerges in this spatial gap within Forster's figure; it is at one with the contradiction between the contingency of physical objects and the demand for an impossible meaning, here marked by dead philosophical abstraction. The solution to this contradiction, which we call "style," is then the substitution of a spatial or perceptual "meaning" (whatever that now is) for the other kind (whatever that was, or might be in the future).

But Forster's figure also turns out to have a more conventional "meaning," as the rest of his novel instructs us: it will be perfectly proper to unravel it, provided we do not lose sight of its initial spatial and perceptual ground, and of the work of some new modernist language on our bodies and our sensorium that is its precondition. He goes on, indeed, to develop his ethos of place, as "the basis of all earthly beauty" (204), which he elaborates into something like a twofold salvation system, the twin paths of intimate human relations and of an immediate landscape: "We want to show him," says Margaret about the wretched Leonard Bast, "how he may get upsides with life. As I said, either friends, or the country, some . . . either some very dear person or some very dear place seems necessary to relieve life's daily grey, and to show that it is grey. If possible, one should have both" (145). The place is of course the country house itself, the Howards End of the title; and the "dear person" the late Mrs. Wilcox, who begins to merge with her dwelling to the point of becoming almost literally a "genius loci." Yet the representational dilemma remains, as in our earlier figure: Mrs. Wilcox as a character draws her possibilities from that concrete place that is Howards End, while this last draws its evocative power from the spirit of Mrs. Wilcox. The transformation of chance encounters ("only connect") into a utopian social community presided over by a woman who is its providential spirit in a virtually literal sense;[10] and the recovery of a utopian landscape orchestrated by the well-nigh Shakespearean glorification of an ideal (and an antipatriotic) England in chapter XIX—the combination, indeed, the identification of these two visionary constructions is Forster's political as well as his aesthetic agenda in his novel.

Yet as he himself makes clear, it is not evident that the operation can be historically realized and completed (even though the novel itself gets written). For he will go on to suggest that the tendential conditions of modern civilization—"modernization" now, rather than aesthetic "modernism"!—are in the process of closing off one of these two avenues of personal and spiritual "salvation" (if that is not too lofty a word for it). Landscape is in the process of being obliterated, leaving only the more fragile and ephemeral safety net of the interpersonal behind it:

> London was but a foretaste of this nomadic civilization, which is altering human nature so profoundly, and throws upon personal relations a stress greater than they have ever borne before. Under cosmopolitanism, if it comes, we shall receive no help from the earth. Trees and meadows and mountains will only be a spectacle, and the binding force that they once exercized on character must be entrusted to Love alone. (261)

But what we must now add, and what now returns us to our starting pint, is that London is very precisely that "infinity" of which we caught a glimpse on the Great North Road, or at least a "caricature" of it (Forster's word, p. 280). But now suddenly a whole set of terms falls into place and begins to

Fredric Jameson

coincide: cosmopolitanism, London, the nomadic, the stench of motorcars, antibilious pills, all begin to coalesce as a single historical tendency, and they are unexpectedly at one with "infinity" itself, which equally unexpectedly becomes the bad opposite of place, of Howards End, of the salvation through the here and the now (and incidentally of the regeneration of some older England that never existed, the utopian England of chapter XIX). But this is not simple romantic antiurban or antimodern nostalgia; it is not at all the conservative revulsion before the faceless industrial masses of the Waste Land, the modern urban world. And that for a final decisive reason, a final identification in this linked chain of phenomena: for infinity in this sense, this new grey placelessness, as well as what prepares it, also bears another familiar name. It is in Forster *imperialism*, or Empire, to give it its period designation. It is Empire which stretches the roads out to infinity, beyond the bounds and borders of the national state, Empire which leaves London behind it as a new kind of spatial agglomeration or disease, and whose commercialism now throws up those practical and public beings, like Mr. Wilcox, around whose repression of the personal Forster's message will also play, taking on new forms we have no time to examine here:

> In the motorcar was another type whom Nature favors — the Imperial. Healthy, ever in motion, it hopes to inherit the earth. It breads as quickly as the yeoman, and as soundly; strong is the temptation to acclaim it as a super-yeoman, who carries his country's virtue overseas. But the Imperialist is not what he thinks or seems. He is a destroyer. He prepares the way for cosmopolitanism, and though his ambitions may be fulfilled, the earth that he inherits will be grey. (323)

With this identification — the coincidence of "infinity" with "imperialism" — we come full circle, and a component of the imperialist situation appears in human form, or in the representational language of a narrative character. Yet the representation is incomplete, and thereby epistemologically distorted and misleading: for we are only able to see that face, the "Imperial type," turn inward, toward the internal metropolitan reality. The other pole of the relationship, what defines him fundamentally and essentially in his "imperial" function—the persons of the colonized— remains structurally occluded, and cannot but so remain, necessarily, as a result of the limits of the system, and the way in which internal national or metropolitan daily life is absolutely sundered from this other world henceforth in thrall to it.[11] But since representation, and cognitive mapping as such, is governed by an "intention towards totality,"[12] those limits must also be drawn back into the system, which marks them by an image, the image of the Great North Road as infinity: a new spatial language, therefore— modernist "style"—now becomes the marker and the substitute (the "tenant-lieu," or place-holding, in Lacanian language) of the unrepresentable totality. With this a new kind of value emerges (and it is this which is generally loosely and misleadingly refered to as modernist aestheticism): for if "infinity" (and "imperialism") is bad or negative in Forster, its perception, as a bodily and poetic process, is no longer that, but rather a positive achievement and an enlargement of our sensorium: so that the beauty of the new figure seems oddly unrelated to the social and historical judgment which is its content.

What I have tried to suggest about this "event" on the border or limit of representation might also have been shown for the representation of inner or metropolitan space itself, for the national daily life which must remain its primary raw material.[13] Because in the imperial world system this last is now radically incomplete, it must by compensation be formed into a self-subsisting totality: something Forster uniquely attempts to achieve by way of his providential ideology, which transforms chance contacts, coincidence, the contingent and random encounters between isolated subjects, into a utopian glimpse of achieved community.

This glimpse is both moral and aesthetic all at once, for it is the achievement of something like an aesthetic pattern of relationships that confirms it as a social reality, however ephemeral; and the coincidence of the social (grasped in moral terms) and the aesthetic is then what allows other related works (such as those of Virginia Woolf) to refocus it by way of operations which look more aestheticizing than Forster's. Here also the internal social totality will remain incomplete; but the internal social classes are nonetheless explicitly designated by their absence (thus, Leonard is carefully characterized as nonproletarian, as standing "at the extreme edge of gentility. He was not in the abyss but he could see it, and at times people whom he knew had dropped in, and counted no more") (45). This internal subsumption is sharply to be distinguished from the exclusion of an external or colonized people (whose absence is not even designated): the distinction would correspond roughly to that which obtains in Freud between repression (neurosis) and foreclusion (psychosis).

The hypothesis suggested here—between the emergence of a properly modernist "style" and the representational dilemmas of the new imperial world system—will be validated only by the kind of new work it enables: by some fresh (formal and structural) approach to the moderns able to formulate their historical specificity more adequately for us today than the descriptions we have inherited from their contemporaries. Yet there is also another way in which such a hypothesis might be "verified," at least by way of an Einsteinian "thought experiment": this would be something like a principle of experimental variation or aesthetic falsifiability, in which this particular metropolitan or First World modernist laboratory experiment is tested against radically different environmental conditions. These are not, in this period, to be found in what will come to be called the Third World, or in the colonies: there the face of imperialism is brute force, naked power, open exploitation; but there also the mapping of the imperialist world system remains structurally incomplete, for the colonial subject will be unable to register the peculiar transformations of First World or metropolitan life which accompany the imperial relationship. Nor will it, from the point of view of the colonized, be of any interest to register those new realities, which are the private concern of the masters, and which a colonized culture must simply refuse and repudiate. What we seek, therefore, is a kind of exceptional situation, one of overlap and coexistence between these two incommensurable realities which are those of the lord and of the bondsman altogether, those of the metropolis and of the colony simultaneously. Our experimental variation, then, would presuppose, were it possible in the first place, a national situation which reproduces the appearance of First World social reality and social relationships—perhaps through the coincidence of its language with the imperial language—but whose underlying structure is in fact much closer to that of the Third World or of colonized daily life. A modernism arising in these circumstances could then be inspected and interrogated for its formal and structural differences from the works produced within the metropolis and examined above. But at least one such peculiar space exists, in the historical contingency of our global system: it is Ireland, and the uniqueness of the Irish situation will now allow us, as it were experimentally, to verify our argument up to this point. For it allows us to make a deduction, as it were, a priori from our hypotheses, and then to compare that deduction with the historical realities of Irish culture. If the thesis is correct, then, we may expect to find, in some abstractly possible Irish modernism, a form which on the one hand unites Forster's sense of the providential yet seemingly accidental encounters of characters with Woolf's aesthetic closure, but which on the other hand projects those onto a radically different kind of space, a space no longer central, as in English life, but marked as marginal and ec-centric after the fashion of the colonized areas of the imperial system. That colonized space may then be expected to transform the modernist formal project radically, while still retaining a distant family likeness to its imperial variants. But this "deduction" finds immediate historical confirmation, for I have in fact been describing *Ulysses*.

But in *Ulysses* space does not have to be made symbolic in order to achieve closure and meaning: its closure is objective, endowed by the colonial situation itself—whence the nonpoetic, nonstylistic nature of Joyce's language. In Forster, the deeper reality of the encounter, the coincidence, the determinate meetings or the five-minute lag that prevents them from coming about, are played off against the metropolis, which "one visualizes as a tract of quivering grey, intelligent without purpose, and excitable without love; as a spirit that has altered before it can be chronicled; as a heart that certainly beats, but with no pulsation of humanity" (108). In Joyce, the encounter is at one with Dublin itself, whose compact size anachronistically permits the now archaic life of the older city-state. It is therefore unnecessary to generate an aesthetic form of closure distinct from the city, which in First World modernism must be imposed by the violence of form upon this last as compensation.

One wants, indeed, to go even further than this and to assert that what has been seen as the linguistic dimension of modernism proper—namely, "style" as such, as something like an absolute category of the modern canon—is also absent in Joyce. The spatial poetry that has been detected in Forster has, for one thing, no equivalent in *Ulysses*. "Am I walking into eternity along Sandymount strand?" is thrust back into Stephen's consciousness, and marked as subjective. At the other end of the continuum, the great anamorphic spaces of the Nighttown chapter take place much too close to the eye, as it were, to be characterized in terms of images. A personal style, evolving toward the conventionally modern, can be detected in early Joyce, and may be identified by way of traces of Walter Pater's mannerisms: all that survives of that in *Ulysses* is the self-conscious placement of crucial adverbs. Otherwise, style, as a category of some absolute subject, here disappears, and Joyce's palpable linguistic games and experiments are rather to be seen as impersonal sentence combinations and variations beyond all point of view ("Love loves to love love. Nurse loves the new chemist. Constable 14A loves Mary Kelly. Gerty McDowell loves the boy that has the bicycle . . . " etc.): whence one's occasional sense that (as with revolutionary modes of production) Joyce leaps over the stage of the modern into full postmodernism. The pastiche of styles in the Oxen of the Sun not merely discredits the category of style as such, but presents an enumeration of *English* styles, of the styles of the imperial occupying armies.

Even the matter of coincidence indeed—so crucial in Forster and Woolf—takes on a different meaning in Joyce, where such intersections are everywhere, but have little of the dubious providentiality they project in our other works (a partial exception needs to be made here for the father-son thematics). Leonard catches sight of Margaret and Mr. Wilcox in Saint Paul's at a climactic moment; Stephen catches sight of Mr. Bloom in a more doubtful, but also more aesthetic moment; yet this last does not raise the same questions as the former. London (or the Manhattan of *Manhattan Transfer*) is an agglomeration (and metropolis) in which such encounters *are* sheer coincidence; Dublin is a classical city in which they are not merely normal but expected. This is to say that a concept of the urban is present in *Ulysses* which contains and motivates those very encounters and intersections crucial to the modern, but lends them a different resonance. But Dublin, as we have said, remains classical because it is also a colonial city: and this "peculiarity" of Joyce's narrative content now determines a certain number of other formal results. For one thing, encounters in Joyce are already (or perhaps I should say, still) linguistic: they are stories, gossip, they have already been assimilated into speech and storytelling while taking place, so that the demiurgic transformation of the modernist poet or writer— the need to invent a new speech in order to render the freshly revealed, nonlinguistic contingencies of modern life—is in Joyce short-circuited. Meanwhile, this essential linguisticality of *Ulysses*—a book, as he said himself, about "the last great talkers"—is itself a result of imperialism, which condemns Ireland to an older rhetorical past and to the survivals of oratory (in the absence of action), and which freezes Dublin into an underdeveloped village in which gossip and rumor still reign supreme. Meanwhile, history itself, which must elsewhere be imported and introduced by fiat, is here already part of the urban fabric: the occupying army is present; it is perfectly natural for us to encounter its soldiers, as it is to witness the viceregal procession; the spasmodic efforts at militancy—such as the assassination of the Invincibles—are still vivid in the collective memory, and the appearance of one of the survivors is a Proustian shock, no doubt, but perfectly plausible. It is normal for the British intelligentsia to visit this interesting cultural backwater; normal for the nationalist debates (very specifically including the one around the national language) to sputter on in pubs, bars, and meeting places; while the very fact of the pub itself, or public space in which you meet and talk, is itself a happy survival of an older urban life, which will have no equivalent in metropolitan literature, where meetings between disparate characters must be more artificially arranged, by means of receptions and summer houses.

Even the one section of *Ulysses* which resembles a rather different modernist approach toward space—the Wandering Rocks, which is the direct inspiration of Dos Passos and his discontinuous literary crosscutting—is the exception that proves the rule, since these palpable discontinuities are already mere appearance: we know already in fact that these disjoined characters are already connected, by acquaintanceship and history, and that a shift in perspective would at once cause the illusion of external chance and coincidence to vanish utterly away. The *Odyssey* parallel itself—which may superficially as an aesthetic design and allusion resemble the painting in Virginia Woolf's *To the Lighthouse*—must also be rethought in the context of imperialism. It is of course the great formal pretext, whose setting in place then allows Joyce to elaborate the contingencies of his individual chapters without any deeper motivation (the other levels of the parallels, the colors, the tropes, the organs of the body, rather resemble Freudian "secondary elaboration" than genuine symbolism): but what must be stressed is that it is not the meaning of the *Odyssey* which is exploited here, but rather its spatial properties. The *Odyssey* serves as a *map*: it is indeed, on Joyce's reading of it, the one classical narrative whose closure is that of the map of a whole complete and equally closed region of the globe, as though somehow the very episodes themselves merged back into space, and the reading of them came to be indistinguishable from map reading. None of the other classical parallels in modern literature has this peculiar spatial dimension (think, for example, of the various subjects of Greek tragedy); indeed, it is as though this Third World modernism slyly turned the imperial relationship inside out, appropriating the great imperial space of the Mediterranean in order to organize the space of the colonial city, and to turn its walks and paths into the closure of a form and of a grand cultural monument.

The traces of imperialism can therefore be detected in Western modernism, and are indeed constitutive of it; but we must not look for them in the obvious places, in content or in representation. Save in the special case of Irish literature, and of Joyce, they will be detected spatially, as formal symptoms, within the structure of First World modernist texts themselves.

NOTES

1. See, for example, Martin Green, *Dreams of Adventure, Deeds of Empire* (New York: Basic Books, 1979); Philip D. Curtin, *The Image of Africa: British Ideas and Action 1780–1850* (Madison: University of Wisconsin Press, 1964); Brian Z. Street, *The Savage in Literature: Representations of "Primitive" Society in English Fiction 1858–1920* (London: Routledge & Kegan

Fredric Jameson

Paul, 1972); and especially Edward W. Said, "*Kim*, the Pleasures of Imperialism," in *Raritan*, 7 (Fall 1987), 27–64, reprinted in his *Culture and Imperialism*.

2. In what follows, the word "metropolis" will designate the imperial nation-state as such, "metropolitan" then applying to its internal national realities and daily life (which are of course not exclusively urban, although organized around some central urban "metropolis" in the narrower sense).

3. Two other essays of mine explore the links between a modernist poetics and what we might today call Third World space: see "Wallace Stevens," *New Orleans Review*, 11 (1984), 10–19, and "Rimbaud and the Spatial Text," in Tak-wai Wong and M. A. Abbas (eds.), *Re-writing Literary History* (Hong Kong: Hong Kong University Press, 1984), 66–93.

4. I draw here essentially on Anthony Brewer's excellent *Marxist Theories of Imperialism: A Critical Survey* (London: Routledge & Kegan Paul, 1980).

5. Bill Warren's *Imperialism: Pioneer of Capitalism* (London: Verso, 1980) may be seen as a contemporary reformulation of these classical positions.

6. The reference is to Edward J. Dudley and Maximilian Novak (eds.), *The Wild Man Within: An Image in Western Thought from the Renaissance to Romanticism* (Pittsburgh: University of Pittsburgh Press, 1973).

7. I am reluctant to repeat here the obligatory knee-jerk condemnations of causality and so-called linear history, although I do not particularly feel that the situation/response model (drawn from Sartre) is a "causal" one in that stereotypical sense.

8. E. M. Forster, *Howards End* (London, 1910; New York: Knopf, 1921), 14–15; henceforth all references given in the text are to this edition.

9. It is, I take it, the position of Terry Eagleton's stimulating *Exiles and Emigrés* (New York: Schocken, 1970) that all the most important modern writers of what we think of as the *English* canon are in fact social marginals of various kinds, when not outright foreigners. The analogy to be explored with Britain is of course the Austro-Hungarian Empire, which was an extraordinarily rich terrain for a variety of the most important modernisms in all the arts (and in philosophy as well). Hugo von Hofmannsthal May here be taken as the nonethnic Austrian norm, from which these modernisms are the deviation: his "Letter from Lord Chandos" is a paradigmatic text about the discovery and subsequent repudiation of the "modern."

10. Formally, the position of Mrs. Wilcox in this novel demands comparison with that of Mrs. Ramsay in Virginia Woolf's *To the Lighthouse*, an analysis of which forms a part of the larger version of the present essay.

11. Africa is set in place by the mediation of Charles Wilcox, who works in Uganda for his father's Imperial and West African Rubber Company (see 195–96). About *A Passage to India*, what needs to be said here is (a) that Forster's luck lay in the fact that one of the many Indian languages is the one called Indian English, which he was able to learn like a foreign language; and (b) that the novel is restricted to British and Muslim characters (Islam being, as Lévi-Strauss instructs us in *Tristes Tropiques*, the last and most advanced of the great *Western* monotheisms), the Hindus

specifically designated as that Other are inaccessible to Western representation.

12. Georg Lukács, *History and Class Consciousness* (Cambridge, Mass.: MIT Press, 1971), 174 (where the German "*Intention*" is translated "*aspiration*").

13. My oldest thoughts on all this were stimulated into being by Gertrude Stein's remarkable "What Is English Literature" in *Lectures in America* (Boston: Beacon, 1985). As this book no longer seems widely read, I will not resist quoting a relevant extract: "If you live a daily life and it is all yours, and you come to own everything outside your daily life besides and it is all yours, you naturally begin to explain. You naturally continue describing your daily life which is all yours and you naturally begin to explain how you own everything besides. You naturally begin to explain that to yourself and you naturally begin to explain it to those living your daily life who own it with you, everything outside, and you naturally explain it in a kind of way to some of those whom you own" (41).

Other works citied in the text:

Paul Baran, *The Political Economy of Growth* (New York: Monthly Review, 1957).

Jacques Berque, *La Dépossession du Monde* (Paris: Seuil, 1964).

Fredric Jameson

YEATS AND
DECOLONIZATION

YEATS AND DECOLONIZATION

EDWARD W. SAID

I

Yeats has now been almost completely assimilated to the canon as well as the discourses of modern English literature, in addition to those of European high modernism. Both of these institutions of course reckon with him as a great modern Irish poet, deeply affiliated and interacting with his native traditions, the historical and political context of his times, and the extraordinarily complex situation of being a poet in Ireland writing in English. Nevertheless, and despite Yeats's obvious and, I would say, settled presence in Ireland, in British culture and literature, and in European modernism, he does present another fascinating aspect: that of the indisputably great *national* poet who articulates the experiences, the aspirations, and the vision of a people suffering under the dominion of an offshore power. From this perspective Yeats is a poet who belongs to a tradition not usually considered his, that of the colonial world ruled by European imperialism now—that is, during the late nineteenth and early twentieth centuries—bringing to a climactic insurrectionary stage, the massive upheaval of anti-imperialist resistance in the colonies, and of metropolitan anti-imperialist opposition that has been called the age of decolonization. If this is not a customary way of interpreting Yeats for those who know a great deal more about him as an Irish European modernist poet of immense stature than I do, then I can only say that he appears to me, and I am sure to many others in the Third World, to belong naturally to the other cultural domain, which I shall now try to characterize. If this also sheds more light on the present status of Yeats's role in postindependence Ireland, then so much the better.

The age of imperialism is conventionally said to have begun in the late 1870s, with the scramble for Africa. Yet it seems to me to be perfectly clear that there are all sorts of cultural as well as political indications that it began a good deal earlier. Even if we speak only about the eighteenth and nineteenth centuries, Britain and France, who dominate the history of European imperialism until World War II (Britain especially), are to be found already present in those very territories that are later to become formally central during the heyday of imperialist ideology. India, North Africa, the Caribbean, Central and South America, many parts of Africa, China and Japan, the Pacific archipelago, Malaysia, Australia, North America, and of course Ireland: all these are sites of contention well before 1870 either between various local resistance groups, or between the European powers themselves; in some cases, India and Africa for instance, the two struggles are going on simultaneously long before 1857, and long before the various European congresses on Africa at the end of the century. The point here is of course that no matter how one wishes terminologically to demarcate high imperialism—that period when everyone in Europe and America believed him-or herself in fact to be serving a high civilizational and commercial cause by having an empire—from earlier periods of overseas conquest, rapac-

Edward W. Said

ity, and scientific exploration, imperialism itself was a continous process for at least a century and a half *before* the scramble for Africa. I don't think it much matters to an Indian or an Algerian that in the first half of the nineteenth century he or she did not belong to the age of imperialism whereas after 1850 both of them did. For both of them their land was and had been dominated by an alien power for whom distant hegemony over nonwhite peoples seemed inscribed by right in the very fabric of European and Western Christian society, whether that society was liberal, monarchical, or revolutionary.

I would also want to say that modern European imperialism itself is a constitutively and a radically different type of overseas domination from all earlier forms. Sheer scale and scope are only part of the difference. Certainly neither Byzantium nor Rome nor Athens nor Baghdad nor Spain and Portugal during the fifteenth and sixteenth centuries controlled anything like the territories controlled by Britain and France during the nineteenth century. The more important differences are first the extraordinary and sustained longevity of the disparity in power between Europe and its possessions, and second, the massively organized rule, which affected the detail and not just the large outlines of life, of that power. By the beginning of the nineteenth century, Europe—and in this Britain leads the way—had begun the industrial transformation of its economies; the feudal and traditional land-holding structures were changing; the new mercantilist pattern of overseas trade, naval power, and colonialist settlement were firmly established; the bourgeois revolution had finally entered its triumphant stage. All these things gave the ascendancy of metropolitan Europe over its far-flung and distant possessions a profile of imposing, and even daunting power. By the beginning of World War I Europe and America held 85 percent of the earth's surface in some sort of colonial subjugation. This, I hasten to add, did not happen in a fit of absentminded whimsy or as a result of a distracted shopping spree.

It came about for a whole series of reasons, which the library of systematic work that now exists on imperialism, beginning with Hobson, Rosa Luxemburg, Schumpeter, and Lenin, has ascribed to largely economic and somewhat ambiguously characterized political processes. My own theory, which I put forth in the book from which these comments are an extract, is that culture played a very important, indeed indispensable role. At the heart of European culture during the many decades of imperial expansion lay what could be called an undeterred and unrelenting Eurocentrism. This accumulated experiences, territories, peoples, histories; it studied them, classified them, verified them; but above all, it subordinated them to the culture and indeed the very idea of white Christian Europe. This cultural process has to be seen if not as the origin and cause, then at least as the vital, informing, and invigorating counterpoint to the economic and political machinery that we all concur stands at the center of imperialism. And it must also be noted that this Eurocentric culture relentlessly codified and observed everything about the non-European or presumably peripheral world, in so thorough and detailed a manner as to leave no item untouched, no culture unstudied, no people and land unclaimed. All of the subjugated peoples had it in common that they were considered to be naturally subservient to a superior, advanced, developed, and morally mature Europe, whose role in the non-European world was to rule, instruct, legislate, develop, and at the proper times, to discipline, war against, and occasionally exterminate non-Europeans.

From these views that were held in Europe and America there was no significant divergence from the Renaissance on, and if it is embarrassing for us to remark that those elements of a society we have long considered to be progressive were, so far as empire was concerned, uniformly retrograde, we still mustn't be afraid to say it. When I say "retrograde" I speak here of advanced writers and artists, of the working class, and of women, groups whose imperialist fervor increased in intensity and perfervid enthusiasm for the acquisition of and sheer bloodthirsty dominance over innumerable niggers, bog dwellers, babus, and wogs, as the competition between various European and American powers also increased in brutality and senseless, even profitless, control.

What enables us to say all of those things retrospectively is the perspective provided for us in the twentieth century by theoreticians, militants, and insurgent analysts of imperialism like Frantz Fanon, Amilcar Cabral, C. L. R. James, Aimé Césaire, Walter Rodney, plus many others like them on the one hand, and on the other, by the great nationalist artists of decolonization and revolutionary nationalism, like Tagore, Senghor, Neruda, Vallejo, Césaire, Faiz, Darwish . . . and Yeats. Yeats, I think, belongs in this group, for all sorts of reasons, although strangely enough he commonly isn't thought of as a natural, or card-carrying, member. But let me return to Yeats and the case for him a little later, so that I can now complete the general sketch I have been attempting hitherto. As imperialism increased in scope and in depth, so too, in the colonies themselves, the resistance mounted. Indeed, I would go so far as to say that just as in Europe the accumulation on a world scale that gathered the colonial domains systematically into the world market economy was supported and enabled by a culture giving empire an ideological license, so too in the overseas imperium there was a massive political, economic, and military resistance that was itself carried forward and informed by an actively provocative and challenging culture of resistance. It has been the substantial achievement of all of the intellectuals, and of course of the movements they worked with, by their historical interpretive, and analytic efforts to have identified the culture of resistance as a cultural enterprise possessing a long tradition of integrity and power in its own right, one *not* simply grasped as a belated reactive response to Western imperialism.

A great deal, but by no means all, of the resistance to imperialism was conducted in the name of nationalism. Nationalism is a word that has been used in all sorts of sloppy and undifferentiated ways, but it still serves quite adequately to identify the mobilizing force that coalesced into resistance against an alien and occupying empire on the part of peoples possessing a common history, religion, and language. Yet for all its success in ridding many countries and territories of colonial overlords, nationalism has remained, in my opinion, a deeply problematic ideological, as well as sociopolitical, enterprise. At some stage in the antiresistance phase of nationalism there is a sort of dependence between the two sides of the contest, since after all many of the nationalist struggles were led by bourgeoisies that were partly formed and to some degree produced by the colonial power; these are the national bourgeoisies of which Fanon spoke so ominously. These bourgeoisies in effect have often replaced the colonial force with a new class-based and ultimately exploitative force; instead of liberation after decolonization one simply gets the old colonial structures replicated in new national terms.

That is one problem with nationalism: its results are written across the formerly colonized world, usually in the fabrics of newly independent states whose pathologies of power as Eqbal Ahmad has called them, bedevil political life even as we speak. The other problem is that the cultural horizons of nationalism are fatally limited by the common history of colonizer and colonized assumed by the nationalist movement itself. Imperialism after all is a cooperative venture. Both the master and the slave participate in it, and both grew up in it, albeit unequally. One of the salient traits of modern imperialism is that in most places it set out quite consciously to modernize, develop, instruct, and civilize the natives. An entire massive chapter in cultural history across five continents grows up out of it. The annals of schools, missions, universities scholarly societies, hospitals in Asia, Africa, Latin America, Europe, and America, fill its

Edward W. Said

pages, and have had the effect over time of establishing the so-called modernizing trends in the colonial regions, as well as muting or humanizing the harsher aspects of imperialist domination — all of them bridging the gap between imperial center and peripheral territories. In paying respect to it, acknowledging the shared and combined experiences that produced many of us, we must at the same time note how at its center it nevertheless preserved the nineteenth-century imperial divide between native and Westerner. The great colonial schools, for example, taught generations of the native bourgeoisie important truths about history, science, culture. And out of that learning process millions grasped the fundamentals of modern life, yet remained subordinate dependents of an authority based elsewhere than in their lives. Since one of the purposes of colonial education was to promote the history of France or Britain, that same education also demoted the native history. There were always the Englands, Frances, Germanys, Hollands as distant repositories of the Word, for all the contradictions developed during the years of productive collaboration. Stephen Dedalus is a famous example of someone who discovers these facts with unusual force.

The culmination of this dynamic of dependence is, I said a moment ago, the resurgent nationalism of the various independence movements. Right across the Third World (including Ireland) in the period from World War I and concluding in the 1940s and 1950s, new national states appear, all of them declaring their independence from the various European powers whose rule of direct domination had for various reasons come to an end. Nationalism in India, Ireland, and Egypt, for example, was rooted in the longstanding struggle for native rights and independence by nationalist parties like the Congress, Sinn Fein, and the Wafd. Similar processes occurred in other parts of Africa and Asia. Nehru, Nasser, Sukarno, Nkrumah: the pantheon of Bandung flourished, in all its suffering and greatness, because of the nationalist dynamic. Crucial works like

Panikkar's *Asia and Western Dominance*, George Antonius's *The Arab Awakening*, and the various works of the Irish revival were produced out of it. Nevertheless, there were two distinct political moments during the nationalist revival, each with its own imaginative culture, the second unthinkable both in politics and history without the first. One was the period of nationalist anti-imperialism; the other, an era of liberationist anti-imperialist resistance that often followed it. The first was a pronounced awareness of European and Western culture *as* imperialism, as a reflexive moment of consciousness that enabled the African, Caribbean, Irish, Latin American, or Asian citizen inching toward independence through decolonization to require a theoretical assertion of the end of Europe's cultural claim to guide and/or instruct the non-European or nonmainland individual. Often this was first done as Thomas Hodgkin has argued "by prophets and priests," among them poets and visionaries, versions perhaps of Hobsbawm's precapitalist protest and dissent. The second more openly liberationist moment occurred during a dramatic prolongation after World War II of the Western imperial mission in various colonial regions, principal among them Algeria, Vietnam, Palestine, Ireland, Guinea, Cuba. Whether in its general statements such as the Indian constitution, or Pan-Arabism and Pan-Africanism, or in its particularist forms such as Pearse's Gaelic or Senghor's *négritude*, the nationalism that formed the initial basis of the second moment stood revealed both as insufficient and yet as an absolutely crucial first step. Out of this paradox comes the idea of liberation, a strong new postnationalist theme that is already implicit in the works of Connolly, Garvey, Marti, Mariategi, and Du Bois, for instance, but sometimes requiring the propulsive infusion of theory and sometimes armed, insurrectionary militancy to bring it forward clearly, and unmistakably.

Let us look closely at the literature of the first of these moments, that of anti-imperialist resistance. Its literature develops quite consciously out of a desire to distance the native

African, Indian, or Irish individual from the British, French, or (later) American master. Before this can be done, however, there is a pressing need for the recovery of the land that, because of the presence of the colonizing outsider, is recoverable at first only through the imagination. Now if there is anything that radically distinguishes the imagination of anti-imperialism it is the primacy of the geographical in it. Imperialism after all is an act of geographical violence through which virtually every space in the world is explored, charted, and finally brought under control. For the native, the history of his or her colonial servitude is inaugurated by the loss to an outsider of the local place, whose concrete geographical identity must thereafter be searched for and somehow restored. From what? Not just from foreigners, but also from a whole other agenda whose purpose and processes are controlled elsewhere.

Let me give three examples of how complex and how totalizing is the geographical *morte main* of imperialism, and, more important, how radical, how heroic is the effort needed somehow to win back control of one's own territory. The first example is offered in a recent study by Alfred Crosby, *Ecological Imperialism: The Biological Expansion of Europe, 900–1900*. Crosby says that wherever they went Europeans immediately began to change the local habitat; their conscious aim was to transform territories in places as far away from Europe as South America and Australia into images of what they left behind. This process was neverending, as a huge number of plants, animals, crops, and farming as well as building methods invaded the colony and gradually turned it into a new place, complete with new diseases, environmental imbalances, and traumatic dislocations for the overpowered natives who had little choice in the matter. A changed ecology also introduced a changed political system that, in the eyes of the nationalist poet or visionary, seemed retrospectively to have alienated the people from their authentic traditions, ways of life, political organizations. A great deal of myth making went into these retrospective decolonizations, by which the land was seen again, revised so to speak, in a state that antedated its alienation by imperialism. But we must not doubt to the extent of the actual changes wrought by imperialism, however much we fault the nationalist poet and writer for his excessive romanticism.

A second example is to be found in an extraordinary book by the Indian political theorist and historian, Ranajit Guha, *A Rule of Property for Bengal*. Guha's study is an account of how the Act of Permanent Settlement for Bengal was enacted in 1826 at the instigation of Philip Francis, a functionary of the East India Company. In a painstaking archaeological investigation of the legal decree that made all the rents in Bengal permanent and uniform, Guha describes the intellectual background in Europe of so important a piece of legislation for India. Francis was a physiocrat; he was also an Englightenment rationalist whose ideas were entirely Western, although they acquired the enforceable status in India of an unbreakable law. Thus to Indians the literal worth of their land in currency and produce was determined by Englishmen whose thought—abstract, rationalistic, inflexible—preempted and then displaced the traditional customs of a complex native society.

My last example also derives from recent research. In his book *Uneven Development* the geographer Neil Smith provides a brilliant formulation of how the production of a particular kind of nature and space under historical capitalism is essential to the unequal development of a landscape that integrates poverty with wealth, industrial urbanization with agricultural diminishment. The culmination of this process is imperialism, which achieves the domination, classification, and universal commodification of all space, under the aegis of the metropolitan center. Its cultural analogue is commerical geography, whose perspectives (for example, in the work of Mackinder and Chisolm) justified imperialism as the result of "natural" fertility or infertility, of available sea lanes, of permanently differentiated zones, territories, climates, and peoples (Smith, 102). Thus is accomplished "the universality of capitalism," which is "the differentiation of national space according to the territorial division of labor" (146).

Following Hegel, Marx, and Lukács, Smith calls the production of this scientifically "natural" world, a *second* nature. To the imagination of anti-imperialism, *our* space at home in the peripheries has been usurped and put to use by outsiders for *their* purpose. It is therefore necessary to seek out, to map, to invent, or to discover, a *third* nature, which is not pristine and prehistorical ("Romantic Ireland's dead and gone," says Yeats) but one that derives historically and abductively from the deprivations of the present. This impulse then is what we might call *cartographic*, and among its most striking examples are Yeats's early poems collected in "The Rose," Neruda's various poems charting the Chilean landscape, Césaire on the Antilles, Faiz on Pakistan, and Darwish on Palestine:

> Restore to me the color of face
> And the warmth of body
> The light of heart and eye,
> The salt of bread and earth . . . the Motherland.
> ("A Lover from Palestine," 23)

With the new territoriality there comes a whole set of further assertions, recoveries, and identifications; all of them quite literally grounded on this poetically projected base. The search for authenticity, for a more congenial national origin than that provided by colonial history, for a new pantheon of heroes, myths, and religions, these too are enabled by the land. And along with these nationalistic adumbrations of the decolonized identity, there always goes an almost magically inspired, quasi-alchemical redevelopment of the native language. Yeats is especially interesting here. He shares with Caribbean and some African writers the predicament of a common language with the colonial overlord, and of course he belongs in many important ways to the Protestant Ascendancy whose Irish loyalties, to put it mildly, were confused. There is, I think, a fairly logical progression then from Yeats's early Gaelicism, with its Celtic preoccupations and themes, to his later systematic mythologies as set down in programmatic poems like "Ego Dominus Tuus" and in the treatise *A Vision*. For Yeats the overlappings he knew existed between his Irish nationalism and the English cultural heritage that both dominated and empowered him as a writer were bound to cause an overheated tension, and it is the pressure of this urgently political and secular tension that one may speculate caused him to try to resolve it on a "higher," that is, nonpolitical level. Thus the deeply eccentric and aestheticized histories he produced in *A Vision* and the later quasi-religious poems are elevations of the tension to an extrawordly level.

In what must stand as the most interesting and brilliant account of Yeats's idea of revolution, Seamus Deane in *Celtic Revivals* has suggested that Yeats's early and invented Ireland was "amenable to his imagination . . . [whereas] he ended by finding an Ireland recalcitrant to it." Whenever Yeats tried to reconcile his occultist views with an actual Ireland—as in "The Statues"—the results, Deane says correctly, are strained. Because Yeats's Ireland was a revolutionary country, Yeats was able to use Ireland's backwardness as the source of its radically disturbing, disruptive return to spiritual ideals that had been lost to an overdeveloped modern Europe. Moreover, in such dramatic realities as the Easter 1916 uprising Yeats also saw the breaking of a cycle of endless, perhaps finally meaningless recurrence, as symbolized by the apparently limitless travails of Cuchulain. Deane's theory therefore is that the birth of an Irish national identity coincides for Yeats with the breaking of the cycle, although it also underscores and reinforces the colonialist British attitude of a specific Irish national character. Thus Yeats's return to mysticism and his recourse to fascism, Deane says perceptively, are underlinings of the colonial predicament to be found, for example, in V. S. Naipaul's representations of India, that of a culture indebted to the mother country for its own self and for a sense of "Englishness" and yet turning toward the colony: "Such a search for a national signature becomes colonial, on account of the different histories of the two islands. The greatest flowering of such a search has been Yeats's poetry." And Deane goes on to conclude that far from representing an outdated nationalism, Yeats's willful mysticism and incoherence do embody a revolutionary potential in the poet's insistence that "Ireland should retain its culture by keeping awake its consciousness of metaphysical questions." In a world from which the harsh strains of capitalism have removed thought and reflection, a poet who can stimulate a sense of the eternal and of death into consciousness is the true rebel, a figure whose colonial diminishments spur him to a negative apprehension of his society and of "civilized" modernity.

The final Adornian formulation of Yeats's quandary as it appears to the contemporary critic is of course powerful and it is attractive. Yet might we not suspect it a little of wanting to excuse Yeats's unacceptable and indigestible reactionary politics—his outright fascism, his fantasies of old homes and families, his incoherently occult divagations—by seeking to translate them into an instance of Adorno's "negative dialectic," thereby rendering Yeats more heroic than a crudely political reading would have suggested? As a small corrective to Deane's conclusion, could we not more accurately see in Yeats a particularly exacerbated example of the *nativist* (e.g., *négritude*) phenomenon, which has flourished elsewhere as a result of the colonial encounter?

Now it is true that the connections are closer between England and Ireland, than between England and India, or France and Senegal. But the imperial relationship is there in all cases. The colonized may have a *sense* of England and France, speak and write in the dominant language even as he or she tries simultaneously to recover a native original, may even act in ways that directly conflict with the overall interests of his/her people, and still the divide remains. This, it seems to me, has always been the case in every colonial relationship, because it is the first principle of imperialism that there is clear-cut and absolute hierarchical distinction between ruler and ruled. Nativism, alas, reinforces the distinction by revaluating the weaker or subservient partner. And it has often led to compelling but often demagogic assertions about a native past, history, or actuality that seems to stand free not only of the colonizer but of worldly time itself. One sees the drive backward in such enterprises as Senghor's *négritude*, or in Soyinka's explorations of the African past, or in the Rastifarian movement, or in the Garveyite solution, or all through the Islamic world, the rediscoveries of various unsullied, precolonial Muslim essences.

Even if we leave aside the tremendous *ressentiment* often to be found in nativism (for example, in Jalal Ali Ahmad's *Occidentosis*) there are two reasons for rejecting, or at least reconceiving, the nativist enterprise. Deane says that it is incoherent and yet, by its negation of politics and history, also heroically revolutionary. That, it seems to me, is to fall into the nativist position too willingly, as if nativism were the only alternative for a resisting and decolonizing nationalism. The main reason therefore to refuse it is rather that we have enough evidence of its ravages elsewhere to regard it today with very much charity: to accept nativism is to accept the consequences of imperialism too willingly, to accept the very radical, religious, and political divisions imposed on places like Ireland, India, Lebanon, and Palestine by imperialism itself. To leave the historical world for the metaphysics of essences like negritude, Irishness, Islam, and Catholicism is, in a word, to abandon history. Most often this abandonment in the postimperial setting has often led to some sort of millenarianism, if the movement has any sort of mass base, or it has degenerated into small-scale private craziness, or into an unthinking acceptance of stereotypes, myths, animosities, and traditions encouraged by imperialism. No one needs to be reminded that such programs are hardly what great resistance movements had imagined as their goals.

The other reason now for tempering the nativist and, in Yeats's case as formulated by Deane, the specifically Irish colonial attitude with a decent admixture of secular skepticism, is of course that nativism is not the only alternative. Here I return to what I said at the outset, that the first moment of resistance to imperialism brought forth all the various nationalist and independence movements that culminated in the large-scale dismantling of the great classical empires, and the birth of many new states throughout the world. The second moment (liberation), however, still continues with us, and its complexities and turbulence in many instances still defy resolution. In this phase, imperialism courses on, as it were, belatedly and in different forms perhaps, but the relationship of domination continues. Even though there was an Irish Free State by the end of his life Yeats in fact partially belonged to this second moment; the evidence for it is his sustained anti-British sentiment. And we know from the experiences of numerous colonial regions—Algeria, Vietnam, Cuba, Palestine, South Africa, and others—that the struggle for release continued. It is in this phase that I would like to suggest that *liberation*, and not nationalist independence, is the new alternative, liberation which by its very nature involves, in Fanon's words, a transformation of social consciousness beyond national consciousness.

From the perspective of liberation then, Yeats's slide into incoherence and mysticism, his rejection of politics, and his arrogant but often charming espousal of fascism (or if not fascism then authoritarianism perhaps even of the South American kind), appear as something not to be excused, something that should not too quickly and alchemically be dialecticized into the negative utopian mode. Later I want to argue that one can quite easily situate and criticize those unacceptable attitudes of Yeats without throwing out the baby with the bath water, without changing one's view of Yeats as a poet of decolonization. But for the moment I should like to make the case that the way beyond nativism is figured in the great turn at the climax of Césaire's *Cahier d'un retour* when the poet realizes that, after the rediscovery and reexperiencing of his past, after reentering the passions, horrors, and circumstances of his history as a black, after feeling and then emptying himself of his anger, after accepting

> J'accepte . . . j'accepte . . . entièrement, sans reserve
> ma race qu'aucune ablution d'hypsope et de lys melés
> ne pourrait purifier
> ma race rongée de macule
> ma race raisin mur pour pieds ivres (72)

> [I accept . . . I accept . . . totally, without reservation
> my race that no ablution of hyssop mixed with lilies
> could purify
> my race pitted with blemishes
> my race a ripe grape for drunken feet]

after all this he is suddenly assailed by strength and life "comme un taureau," and begins to understand that

> il n'est point vrai que l'oeuvre de l'homme est finie
> que nous n'avons rien à faire au monde
> que nous parasitions le monde
> qu'il suffit que nous mettions au pas du monde mais
> L'oeuvre de l'homme vient seulment de commencer
> et il reste à l'homme à conquérir toute interdiction
> immobilisée aux coins de sa ferveur et aucune race
> ne possède le monopole de la beauté, de l'intelligence,
> de la force

> et il est place pour tous au rendez-vous de la conquête
> et nous nous savons maintenant que le soleil tourne
> autour de notre terre eclairant la parcelle qu'a fixée
> notre volonté seule et que toute étoile chute de ciel
> en terre à notre commandement sans limite. (76)

[for it is not true that the work of man is done
that we have no business being on earth
that we parasite the world
that it is enough for us to heel to the world
whereas the work has only begun
and man still must overcome all the interdictions
wedged in the recesses of his fervor and no race has a
monopoly on beauty, on intelligence, on strength

and there is room for everyone at the convocation of
conquest and we know now that the sun turns around
our earth lighting the parcel designated by our will
alone and that every star falls from sky to earth at our
omnipotent command.]

The striking part of this are phrases like "à conquérir toute
interdiction immobilisée aux coins de sa ferveur" and "le
soleil . . . eclairant la parcelle qu'a fixée notre volonté
seule." You don't give in to the rigidity and interdictions of
those self-imposed limitations that come with race, moment, or milieu; instead you move through them to an ani-
mated and expanded sense of "le rendez-vous de la con-
quête," which necessarily involves more than your Ireland,
your Martinque, your Pakistan, etc.

I don't mean to use Césaire *against* Yeats (or Seamus
Deane's Yeats), but rather more fully to associate a major
strand in Yeats's poetry both with the poetry of decolonization and resistance, and with the historical alternatives to
the nativist impasse. For in so many other ways Yeats is very
much the same as other poets resisting imperialism, in his
insistence on a new narrative for his people, his anger at the
schemes for partition (and enthusiasm for its felt opposite,
the requirement of wholeness), the celebration and com-
memoration of violence in bringing about a new order, and
the sinuous interweaving of loyalty and betrayal in the nationalist setting. Yeats's direct association with Parnell and
O'Leary, with the Abbey Theatre, with the Easter Uprising,

brings to his poetry what R. P. Blackmur, borrowing from Jung, calls "the terrible ambiguity of an immediate experience." As one reads Yeats's work in the early 1920s, there is an uncanny resemblance to the engagement and ambiguities of Darwish's Palestinian poetry half a century later, in *its* renderings of violence, of the overwhelming suddenness and surprises of historical events, of the role of politics and poetry, as opposed to violence and guns (see "Roses and Dictionaries"), of the search for respites after the last border has been crossed, the last sky flown in. "The holy centaurs of the hills are vanished," says Yeats sixty years earlier, "I have nothing but the embittered sun."

One feels in reading poems like "Nineteen Hundred and Nineteen" or "Easter 1916," and "September 1913," not just the disappointments of life commanded by "the greasy till" or the violence of roads and horses, of "weasels fighting in a hole," but also of a terrible new beauty that changes utterly the old political and moral landscape. Like all the poets of decolonization Yeats struggles to announce the contours of an "imagined" or ideal community, crystallized not only by its sense of itself but also of its enemy. Imagined community, Benedict Anderson's fine phrase for emergent nationalism, is apt here as I have used it, so long as we are not obliged to accept his mistakenly linear periodizations of unofficial and official nationalism. In the cultural discourses of decolonization, a great many languages, histories, forms, circulate. As Barbara Harlow has shown in *Resistance Literature*, there are spiritual autobiographies, poems of protest, prison memoirs, didactic dramas of deliverance, but in them all is a sense of the instability of time, which has to be made and remade by the people and its leaders. The shifts in Yeats's accounts of his great cycles invoke this instability, as does the easy commerce in his poetry between popular and formal speech, folk tale, and learned writing. The disquiet of what T. S. Eliot called the "cunning history, [and] contrived corridors" of time—the wrong turns, the overlap, the senseless repetition, the occasionally glorious mo-

ment—furnish Yeats, as they do all the poets of decolonization with stern martial accents, heroism, and the grinding
persistence of "the uncontrollable mystery on the bestial
floor."

II

In the first volume of his
memoirs Neruda speaks of a writer's congress in Madrid
held in 1937 in defense of the Republic. "Priceless replies"
to the invitations "poured in from all over. One was from
Yeats, Ireland's national poet; another, from Selma Lagerlof,
the notable Swedish writer. They were both too old to travel
to a beleaguered city like Madrid, which was steadily being
pounded by bombs, but they rallied to the defense of the
Spanish Republic" (*Memoirs*, 130). This passage comes as a
surprise to someone who like myself had once been influ-
enced by Conor Cruise O'Brien's famous account of Yeats's
politics, an essay whose claims are, it seems to me, hope-
lessly inadequate when contrasted with the information and
analysis put forward by Elizabeth Cullingford's *Yeats, Ireland
and Facism* (which also refers to the Neruda recollection).
Just as Neruda saw no difficulty in thinking of himself as a
poet who dealt both with internal colonialism in Chile and
with external imperialism throughout Latin America, we
should think of Yeats, I believe, as an Irish poet with more than
strictly local Irish meaning and applications. Neruda takes him
as a national poet who represents the Irish nation in its war
against tyranny, and, according to Neruda, Yeats responded
positively to that unmistakably antifascist call, despite his frequently cited dispositions toward European fascism.

There is a justly famous poem, "El pueblo," by Neruda in
the 1962 collection *Plenos Poderos* (a collection translated
by Alistair Reid, whose version I have used, as *Fully Empow-*

ered). The resemblance between Neruda's poem and Yeats's "The Fisherman" is striking, because in both poems the central figure is an anonymous man of the people, who in his strength and loneliness is also a mute expression *of* the people; and it is this quality that inspires the poet in his work. Yeats: It is long since I began / To call up to the eyes / This wise and simple man. / All day I'd look in the face / What I had hoped 'twould be / To write for my own race / And the reality." Neruda:

> I knew that man, and when I could
> when I still had eyes in my head,
> when I still had a voice in my throat,
> I sought him among the tombs and I said to him,
> pressing his arm that still was not dust:
> "Everything will pass, you will still be living.
> You set fire to life.
> You made what is yours."
> So let no one be perturbed when
> I seem to be alone and am not alone;
> I am not without company and I speak for all.
> Someone is hearing me without knowing it,
> But those I sing of, those who know,
> go on being born and will overflow the world. (131)

The poetic calling develops out of a pact made between people and poet; hence the power of such invocations to an actual poem as those provided by the popular but silent figures both men seem to require. But the chain does not stop there, since Neruda goes on (in "Deber del Poeta") to claim that "through me, freedom and the sea / will call in answer to the shrouded heart," and Yeats in "The Tower" speaks of sending imagination forth "and call images and memories / From ruins or from ancient trees." Yet because such protocols of exhortation and expansiveness are announced from under the shadow of domination, we would not be wrong to connect them with the new, and perhaps even under-

Edward W. Said

ground narrative of liberation depicted so memorably in Fanon's *Wretched of the Earth*. For whereas the divisions and separations of the colonial order freeze the population's captivity into a sullen torpor, "new outlets . . . engender aims for the violence of colonized peoples" (59). Fanon specifies such things as declarations of human rights, clamors for free speech, trades union demands; later, as the violent confrontation escalates, there is an entirely new history that unfolds subterraneously, as a revolutionary class of militants, drawn from the ranks of the urban poor, the outcasts, criminals, and *declassés*, takes to the countryside, there slowly to form cells of armed activists, who return to the city for the final stages of the insurgency.

The extraordinary power of Fanon's writing is that it is presented as a surreptitious counternarrative to the aboveground force of the colonial regime, which in the teleology of Fanon's narrative is certain to be defeated. The difference between Fanon and Yeats is, I think, that Fanon's theoretical and perhaps even metaphysical narrative of anti-imperialist decolonization is cadenced and stressed from beginning to end with the accents and inflections of liberation. Fanon's is a discourse of that anticipated triumph, liberation, which marks the second moment of decolonization. Yeats, on the other hand, is a poet whose early work sounds the nationalist note and stands finally at the very threshold it cannot actually ever cross. Yet it is not wrong to interpret Yeats as in his poetry setting a trajectory in common with other poets of decolonization, like Neruda and Darwish, which he could not complete, even though perhaps they could go further than he did. This at least gives him credit for adumbrating the liberationist and utopian revolutionism in his poetry that had been belied, and to some extent canceled out, by his late reactionary politics.

It is interesting that Yeats has often been cited in recent years as someone whose poetry warned of nationalist excesses. He is quoted without attribution, for example, in Gary Sick's book (*All Fall Down*) on the Carter administration's handling of the Iranian hostage crisis in 1979–81; and I can distinctly recall that the *New York Times* correspondent in Beirut in 1975–76, James Markham, quotes the same passages from "The Second Coming" in a piece he did about the onset of the Lebanese civil war in 1977. "Things fall apart; the centre cannot hold" is one phrase. The other is "The best lack all conviction, while the worst / Are full of passionate intensity." Sick and Markham both write as Americans frightened of the revolutionary tide sweeping through a Third World once contained by Western power. Their use of Yeats is minatory: remain orderly, or you're doomed to a frenzy you cannot control. As to how, in an inflamed colonial situation, the colonized are supposed to remain orderly and civilized—given that the colonial order has long since profited the oppressor and has long since been discredited in the eyes of the colonized—neither Sick nor Markham tells us. They simply assume that Yeats, in any event, is on our side, *against* the revolution. It's as if both men could never have thought to take the current disorder back to the colonial intervention itself, which is what Chinua Achebe does in 1958, in his great novel *Things Fall Apart*.

The point, I believe, is that Yeats is at his most powerful precisely as he imagines and renders that very moment itself. His greatest decolonizing works quite literally conceive of the birth of violence, or the violent birth of change, as in "Leda and the Swan," instants at which there is a blinding flash of simultaneity presented to his colonial eyes—the girl's rape, and alongside that, the question "did she put on his knowledge with his power / Before the indifferent beak could let her drop?" Yeats situates himself at that juncture where the violence of change is unarguable, but where the results of the violence beseech necessary, if not always sufficient, reason. More precisely, Yeats's greatest theme in the poetry that culminates in *The Tower* is, so far as decolonization is concerned, how to reconcile the inevitable violence of the colonial conflict with the everyday politics of an ongoing national struggle, and also with the power of each of the various parties in the colonial conflict, with the discourse of reason, of persuasion, of organization, with the requirements of poetry. Yeats's prophetic perception that at some point violence cannot be enough and that the strategies of politics and reason must come into play is, to my knowledge, the first important announcement in the context of decolonization of the need to balance violent force with an exigent political and organizational process. Fanon's assertion, almost half a century later than Yeats, that the liberation cannot be accomplished simply by seizing power (though he says, "Even the wisest man grows tense with some sort of violence"), underlines the importance of Yeats's insight. That neither Yeats nor Fanon offers a prescription for undertaking the transition from direct force to a period *after* decolonization when a new political order achieves moral hegemony, is part of the difficulty we live with today in Ireland, Asia, Africa, the Caribbean, Latin America, and the Middle East.

How one can assure the marriage of knowledge to power, or of understanding with violence is a theme in Gramsci's work, undertaken and elaborated in a wholly different context. In the Irish colonial setting, Yeats can only pose and repose the question provocatively, using his poetry, Blackmur says, as a technique of trouble. Yeats goes somewhat further than asking questions, however, in great poems of summation and vision like "Among School Children," "The Tower," "A Prayer for My Daughter," "Under Ben Bulben," and "The Circus Animals' Desertion." These are poems most emininently of genealogy and recapitulation of course. In the colonial context their significance is that they reverse the slenderizing, the reductiveness, and the slanderous encapsulation of Irish actualities that, according to a very learned book by Joseph Leerssen (*Mere Irish and Fior-Ghael*), had been the fate of the Irish at the hands of English writers for eight centuries. Displacing ahistorical rubrics such as "potato-eaters" or "bog-dwellers" or "shanty people," Yeats's poetry joins his people to its history, the more imperatively in that as father, or as "sixty year old smiling public man," or as son and husband, the poet assumes that the narrative and the density of personal experience are equivalent to the experience of his people. The range of references in the closing strophes of "Among School Children," suggests that Yeats was reminding his audience that history and the nation were not separable, any more than a dancer was separate from the dance.

The power of Yeats's accomplishment in restoring a suppressed history, and rejoining the nation to it, is rendered dramatic when we recall Fanon:

> Colonialism is not satisfied merely with holding a people in its grip and emptying the native's brain of all form and content. By a kind of perverted logic, it turns to the past of the people, and distorts, disfigures and destroys it. (210)

What the efforts of Mangan, Ferguson, and Davis did in the field of cultural nationalism, Yeats does after them in another, more challenging way. He rises from the level of personal experience to that of national archetype, without losing the immediacy of the former or the stature of the latter. Moreover, Yeats's unerring choice of genealogical fables and figures speaks to another aspect of colonialism, as described by Fanon: its capacity for separating the individual from his or her own instinctual life, thereby breaking the generative lineaments of the national identity:

> On the unconscious plane, colonialism therefore did not seek to be considered by the native as a gently loving mother who protects her child from a hostile environment, but rather as a mother who unceasingly restrains her fundamentally perverse offspring from managing to commit suicide and from giving free rein to its evil instincts. The colonial mother protects her child from itself,

Edward W. Said

from its ego, and from its physiology, its biology, and its own unhappiness which is its very essence.

In such a situation the claims of the native intellectual [and poet] are not a luxury but a necessity in any coherent program. The native intellectual who takes up arms to defend his nation's legitimacy, who is willing to strip himself naked to study the history of his body, is obliged to dissect the heart of his people. (211)

No wonder that Yeats instructed Irish poets to

> Scorn the sort now growing up
> All out of shape from toe to top,
> Their unremembering hearts and heads
> Base-born products of base beds.

That in the process, again according to Blackmur, Yeats ended up creating not individuals but types that "cannot quite overcome the abstractions from which they sprang" (118) is true to the extent that the decolonizing program and its background in the history of Ireland's subjugation are ignored, as Blackmur was wont to do in interpreting poetry so masterfully and yet so ahistorically. When the colonial realities are taken into account we get "insight and experience," and not merely "the allegorical simulacrum churned with action" (119). I will confess, however, that Yeats's full system of cycles, pernes, and gyres in any case seems important only as it symbolizes his understandable attempts to lay hold of an extremely distant and extremely orderly reality felt as a refuge from the colonial turbulence before his eyes. And when in the Byzantium poems he asks to be gathered into the artifice of eternity, the need for respite from age and from what we would later call "the struggle of the fly in marmalade" is even more starkly at work. Otherwise it is difficult to read most of Yeats and not feel that the devastating anger and genius of Swift were harnessed by him to lifting the burdens of Ireland's colonial afflictions. True,

Yeats stopped short of imagining the full political liberation he might have aspired toward, but we are left with a considerable achievement in decolonization nonetheless.

REFERENCES

Achebe, Chinua. *Things Fall Apart* (Harlow: Longman, 1981).

Ahmad, Jalil Ali. *Occidentosis: A Plague from the West* (Berkeley: Mizan Press, 1984).

Anderson, Benedict. *Imagined Communities: Reflections on the Origin and Spread of Nationalism* (London: Verso/ NLB, 1983).

Antinous, George. *The Arab Awakening* (London: Hamish Hamilton, repr. 1938 ed., 1969).

Blackmur, R. P. *Selected Essays of R. P. Blackmur*, ed. D. Donoghue (New York: Ecco Press, 1985).

Cabral, Amilcar. *Return to the Source: Selected Speeches by Amilcar Cabral* (New York and London: Monthly Review Press, 1973).

Césaire, Aimé. *The Collected Poetry of Aimé Césaire*, trans. C. Eshleman and A. Smith (Berkeley: University of California Press, 1983).

Crosby, Alfred W. *Ecological Imperialism: The Biological Expansion of Europe, 900–1900* (Cambridge: Cambridge University Press, 1986).

Cullingford, E. *Yeats, Ireland and Fascism* (New York: New York University Press, 1981).

Darwish, Mahmud. *Victims of a Map*, trans. A. al-Udhari (London: Al Saqi Books, 1984).

Deane, Seamus. *Celtic Revivals: Essays in Modern Irish Literature, 1880–1980* (London: Faber, 1985).

Du Bois, W. E. B. *Colour and Democracy: Colonies and Peace* (New York: Harcourt, Brace, 1945).

Faiz, Faiz Ahmad. *Poems by Faiz*, trans. V. G. Kiernan (London: Allen & Unwin, 1971).

   The True Subject: Selected Poems of Faiz Ahmad Faiz, trans. N. Lazard (Princeton: Princeton University Press, 1988).

Fanon, Frantz. *The Wretched of the Earth* (New York: Grove Press, 1965).

Garvey, Marcus. *Philosophy and Opinions of Marcus Garvey*, 2 vols. (New York: Faro Press, 1968–69).

Gramsci, Antonio. *Antonio Gramsci: Selections from Political Writings 1910–1920*, trans. J. Matthews (New York: International Publishers, 1977).

Guha, Ranajit. *A Rule of Property for Bengal: An Essay on the Idea of Permanent Settlement* (Paris: Mouton, 1963).

Harlow, Barbara. *Resistance Literature* (New York and London: Methuen, 1987).

James, C. L. R. *The Future in the Present: Selected Writings* (Westport, Conn.: L. Hill, 1977).

Mariategui, José. *Seven Interpretive Essays in Peruvian Reality*, trans. M. Urquidi (Austin: University of Texas Press, 1971).

Martí, José. *José Martí; Major Poems*, trans. E. Randall (New York: Holmes and Randal, 1982).

Martí on the USA, selected and trans. L. A. Baralt (Carbondale: Southern Illinois University Press, 1966).

Neruda, Pablo. *Fully Empowered*, trans. A. Reed (New York: Farrar, Straus & Giroux, 1975).

O'Brien, C. C. *Writers and Politics* (New York: Pantheon, 1965).

Panikkar, K. M. *Asia and Western Dominance: A Survey of the Vasco da Gama epoch of Asian History 1498–1943*. New ed. (London: Allen & Unwin, 1965).

Rodney, Walter. *How Europe Underdeveloped Africa* (Washington, D.C.: Howard University Press, 1972).

Senghor, L. S. *Négritude et Humanisme* (Paris: Editions du Seuil, 1964).

Smith, Neil. *Uneven Development: Nature, Capital and the Production of Space* (Oxford: Basil Blackwell, 1984).

INDEX

INDEX

Compiled by Robin Jackson

Achebe, Chinua, 90
Africa: colonization of, 44, 70–71
Ahmad, Eqbal, 74
Ahmad, Jalal Ali, 82
All Fall Down (Sick), 89–90
Antonius, George, 76
Arab Awakening, The (Antonius), 76
Arnold, Matthew, 8, 9, 12, 33
Asia and Western Dominance
    (Panikkar), 76

Baran, Paul, 47–48
Baudelaire, Charles, 54, 55
Beckett, Samuel, 10, 15
Benjamin, Walter, 26
Berkeley, Bishop George, 15
Berque, Jacques, 50
Blackmur, Richard P., 91, 93
Burke, Edmund, 11, 15, 33, 34

Cabral, Amilcar, 73
Cahier d'un retour (Césaire), 84–85
Capitalism: and imperialism, 46–47;
    and modernism, 35
Carlyle, Thomas, 8
Celtic Revivals (Deane), 80–85

Césaire, Aimé, 73, 79, 84–85
Coleridge, Samuel Taylor, 8, 9, 34
Collins, Michael, 27
Colonialism: and loss of meaning,
    50–51; and naming, 11, 17–19;
    and otherness, 12; and
    postmodernism, 18–19. *See also*
    Imperialism
Community: E. M. Forster and, 58;
    and stereotypes, 12–13; Yeats
    and, 86
Connolly, James, 76
Conrad, Joseph, 9, 44, 52
Crosby, Alfred, 77
Cullingford, Elizabeth, 87
Culture: and bourgeois economy,
    36; as imperialism, 76; liberal
    humanist notion of, 33;
    nationalist, 28; and nature, 17;
    proletarian, 28
Culture and Anarchy (Arnold), 33

Darwish, Mahmud, 73, 79, 86, 89
Davies, Sir John, 8
Deane, Seamus, 17, 80–85
Débâcle, La, 49

Dedalus, Stephen, 27, 61, 75
Dos Passos, John, 63
Double Cross (Kilroy), 14
Du Bois, W. E. B., 76

*Ecological Imperialism: The
    Biological Expansion of Europe,
    900–1900* (Crosby), 77
*Eighteenth Brumaire of Louis
    Bonaparte, The* (Marx), 27
Eliot, T. S., 9, 54, 86
Ellis, Havelock, 12
Enlightenment: concept of universal
    equality, 30–34; rationalism in
    India, 78; view of individual, and
    Ireland, 4

Faiz, Faiz Ahmad, 73, 79
Fanon, Frantz, 73, 83, 89, 91, 92
Feminism, 23–24, 34
*Field Day Anthology of Irish Writing,
    The*, 14, 15, 18
Field Day Theatre Company, 6–7, 10,
    14–15, 17
Finnegans Wake (Joyce), 36
Ford, Ford Madox, 9
Forster, E. M., 9, 52–60; and
    community, 58; and failure of
    liberalism, 5; and Joyce, 61-64;
    and xenophobia, 49
Foucault, Michel, 27
Freud, Sigmund, 59, 64
Friel, Brian, 14, 18

Galton, Sir Francis, 12
Garvey, Marcus, 76
Goldsmith, Oliver, 15
Gramsci, Antonio, 32, 91
Guha, Ranajit, 78

Habermas, Jürgen, 29; and
    poststructuralism, 34
Haggard, Rider, 44
Harlow, Barbara, 86
Heaney, Seamus, 17
Heart of Darkness (Conrad), 52
Hegel, Georg Wilhelm Friedrich, 28,
    36, 38, 79

Hegemony: Gramsci's notion of, 32
Heidegger, Martin, 52
Hilferding, Rudolf, 47
History: writing of European, 12–13
Hobsbawm, Eric John, 76
Hobson, John Atkinson, 72
Hodgkin, Thomas, 76
Howards End (Forster), 49, 52–60
Hugo, Victor, 45

Imperialism: age of, 70; and
    cooperation of master and slave,
    74; and culture of resistance to,
    73–77; and ecology, 56, 77–69;
    and Eurocentrism, 72; in Latin
    America, 87; literature of, 9, 44;
    and modernism, 43–66; notions
    of, 48–49; and space, 50–60, 79;
    theories of, 45–48, 72–73. See
    also Africa; Ireland; Nationalism;
    Nativism
Ireland: and the aesthetic, 32–35;
    and British law, 16–17; cultural
    identity in, 24–25, 80; and Dublin
    as colonial city, 62–63; language,
    10; literature in, 4, 11, 13, 17, 76;
    modernism and, 35, 60–64;
    nationalism in, 4, 6–7, 28, 75;
    Northern, 3, 6, 8, 14, 15–17, 18;
    religion and, 13, 24–25; and
    search for origin, 17. See *also*
    Imperialism; Nationalism; Joyce;
    Yeats

James, Cyril Lionel Robert, 73
Joyce, James, 4, 5, 14, 15, 24, 35–36;
    and language revival, 10–11; and
    postmodernism, 61–62; and style,
    61–64. See *also Finnegans Wake*;
    Stephen Dedalus; *Ulysses*

Keats, John, 11
Kierkegaard, Søren, 38
Kilroy, Thomas, 14, 188
Kipling, Rudyard, 9, 44
Kristeva, Julia, 23–24
Lacan, Jacques, 58
Lawrence, D. H., 9

Leavis, Frank Raymond, 9
Leerssen, Joseph, 91
Lenin, Vladimir Ilich, 48, 72; on
    imperialism, 46, 47
Literature: and cinematographic
    perception, 53; experimental
    forms in, 4–5, 35; Latin
    American, 48; and modernism, 9.
    See also Joyce; *Finnegans Wake*;
    Ulysses; Yeats
Literature and Revolution (Trotsky),
    28
Lombroso, Cesare, 12
Lukács, Georg, 79
Luxemburg, Rosa, 47, 72

Making History (Friel), 14
Mallarmé, Stéphane, 45
Mariategi, José, 76
Markham, James, 90
Martí, José, 76
Marx, Karl, 76, 79; and alienation,
    23, 37; on future of socialism,
    26–29; and theories of
    imperialism, 45–47
Mere Irish and Fíor-Ghael (Leerssen),
    91
Metropolis, 44, 56–58, 65 n. 2
Milton, John, 11
Modernism: and capitalism, 35; and
    imperialism, 35; Irish, 60–64; and
    literature, 9; politics of, 45
Moore, George, 10

Naipaul, V. S., 81
Nationalism, British, 7–8; and
    feminism, 29–30; and language,
    10, 79; and naming, 11, 14,
    17–19; and national character, 9,
    11–14; and national identity, 4,
    24–25; and notions of the
    "other," 12; and religion, 8, 13,
    24–25; as resistance to
    imperialism, 74–77, 81–82. *See
    also* Imperialism; Nativism;
    Radicalism
Nationalism, Irish, 4

Nativism: imperial, 9; and
    liberation, 74–77, 81–82; and
    Yeats, 5, 13, 14
Nature: and culture, 17; and
    imperialism, 56, 77–79
Neruda, Pablo, 73, 79, 89; and Yeats,
    87–88
Nordau, Max Simon, 12

O'Brien, Conor Cruise, 87
Occidentosis (Jalal Ali Ahmad), 82
Odyssey, 63–64

Paine, Tom, 34
Paisley, Ian, 8
Panikkar, Kavalam Madhava, 75
Pater, Walter, 61
Paulin, Tom, 14, 17, 18
Pearse, Padraic, 76
Pope, Alexander, 11
Postmodernism: and perception,
    18–19, 43, 53, 61–62
Powell, Enoch, 8

Race: and theories of racial
    degeneration, 12
Radicalism, 26–38. *See also*
    Nationalism
Religion: and national identity, 8, 13,
    24–25
Renan, Ernest, 12
Resistance Literature (Harlow), 86
Riot Act, The (Paulin), 14
Rodney, Walter, 47, 73
Romanticism: and radicalism, 31;
    and the subject, 28
Rule of Property for Bengal, A, 78

Schumpeter, Joseph Alois, 45, 72
Second Generation, 23
Senghor, Leopold Sedar, 73, 76, 82
Shakespeare, William, 11
Shaw, George Bernard, 10, 12, 15
Sick, Gary, 89–90
Smith, Neil, 78–79
Socialism: and individualism, 31
Soyinka, Wole, 82
Spenser, Edmund, 8

Stein, Gertrude, 66
Style: modernist, 53–59. *See also* Joyce
Subject: and global imperialism, 3–5; ideal revolutionary, 37–38; imperial, 48; national, 28–29
Swift, Jonathan, 11, 15, 93
Symbolism, 45
Synge, John Millington, 10

Tagore, Rabindranath, 73
Temple, Sir William, 8
Theater: "translation" in, 14. *See also* Field Day Theatre Company
Things Fall Apart (Achebe), 90
Third World: notions of the, 47–49. *See also* Imperialism; Nationalism
To the Lighthouse (Woolf), 63, 65 n. 9
Totalization: and Joyce, 36
Translations (Friel), 14
Trotsky, Leon, 28

Ulysses (Joyce), 34–36, 52; and colonized space, 61–64; and concept of the urban, 62
Uneven Development (Smith), 78–79

Vallejo, Cesar, 73
Verne, Jules, 44
Vision, A, (Yeats), 80

Wells, H. G., 44
Wilde, Oscar, 10, 31
Williams, Raymond, 23
Wollstonecraft, Mary, 34
Woolf, Virginia, 59, 60, 62, 63
Wretched of the Earth (Fanon), 89

Yeats, William Butler, 5–6, 10–11, 15, 69–95; and fascism, 34, 80–88; and nativism, 5, 13, 14
Yeats, Ireland and Fascism (Cullingford), 87

Zola, Émile, 49

Terry Eagleton is a fellow of Linacre College, Oxford, and lecturer in critical theory at the University of Oxford. He previously was a fellow and tutor in English at Wadham College, Oxford. His books include *Literary Theory* (Minnesota, 1983), *The Rape of Clarissa: Writing, Sexuality, and Class Struggle in Samuel Richardson* (Minnesota, 1982), *Walter Benjamin*, *Criticism and Ideology*, and *Marxism and Literary Criticism*. He is also the author of a novel about James Connolly, *Saints and Scholars*, and a Field Day play about Oscar Wilde, *Saint Oscar*.

Fredric Jameson is the William A. Lane, Jr., Professor of Comparative Literature and director of the Program in Literature and Theory at Duke University. He previously taught at Harvard University, the University of California (San Diego and Santa Cruz), and Yale University. Jameson's books include *The Ideologies of Theory* (Minnesota, 1988), *The Political Unconscious*, *Sartre: The Origins of a Style*, *Marxism and Form*, and *The Prison-House of Language*. He is also a co-editor of the journal *Social Text*.

Edward W. Said is Old Dominion Foundation Professor in the Humanities at Columbia University. He is author of *Orientalism* (nominated for the National Book Critics' Circle Award), *The Question of Palestine*, *Covering Islam*, *The World, the Text, and the Critic*, and *After the Last Sky: Palestinian Lives*.

Seamus Deane is professor of Modern English and American Literature at University College, Dublin, Ireland. His books include *Selected Poems*, *Celtic Revivals*, *A Short History of Irish Literature*, and *The French Enlightenment and Revolution in England, 1789–1832*. Deane is general editor of the forthcoming *Field Day Anthology of Irish Writing, 500–1990*.